THE TRAEGER GRILL BIBLE

over 2000 days of sizzle and smoke with your Traeger. The updated cookbook with complete smoker recipes to become the king of the grill in no time!

Mason Ember

Table of Contents

Chapter 12: Conclusion

12.1 Conversions

12.2 Index

Chapter 1: Introduction

Welcome to The Traeger Grill Bible

Are you ready to become a grill wizard? Here you are, thanks to the magic of your versatile Traeger Grill. Whether you're just starting out or you've got years of grill experience under your belt, this cookbook is packed with everything you need to know and cook up a storm that'll have your loved ones begging for more. Traeger Grills flipped the script on outdoor cooking by rolling out the world's first wood pellet grill. Say goodbye to boring old charcoal or gas setups – Traeger Grills use natural hardwood pellets to infuse your food with that unbeatable smoky goodness. With these grills, you've got the power to grill, smoke, bake, roast, braise, and BBQ like a pro. And here's the kicker:

Consistent Temperature Control: High quality cooking experience. What sets Traeger Grills apart is their ability to achieve an even heat distribution and consistent results.

Versatility: Now from grilling steaks to slow cooking of briskets, from baking cakes and pies to roasting assortment of vegetables, Traeger Grills are all set for all of it.

Wood-Fired Flavor: The natural hardwood pellets are here, and they make your food cravings extraordinary by offering flavors that cannot be obtained by regular grilling.

Ease of Use: Apart from its digital and timer control and automated feeding system, making use of a Traeger Grill is extremely easy when cooking outdoors.

BBQ and smoking are two methods of preparing foods that have been around for centuries and they both have their own specialties in terms of flavors and outcomes. Grilling, on the other hand, entails preparing food using direct heat from a heat source such as a grill. It is especially appropriate for foods that do not require a long time in the oven, for example, steaks, burgers, and vegetables. Grilling is the process where food is cooked directly on a hot surface typically with high heat for a short time where the outside of the food is cooked to a crisp while the inside remains moist. The high heat also imparts a wonderful smokiness that works well with the actual flavors of your ingredients, which is such a treat every time.

However, smoking is a slower and more controlled process of food preparation where food is exposed to low temperature and smoke for an extended period using indirect heat. This technique works best for large pieces of meat such as briskets, ribs, and pork butts. The smoke has ample time to soak through the meat and create that deep, smoky flavor that makes this cut so delicious; the end results are tender and juicy. In addition to the flavoring, the smoking process adds a specific texture that is tender and juicy. The knowledge of these two concepts of grilling and smoking will enable one to decide on which method is suitable for a particular dish that they are preparing, and this will enable one to get the best results when using Traeger Grill.

1.2 Essential Tools and Accessories

It is important to note that to fully maximize the potential of your Traeger Grill and to make your grilling and smoking experience as smooth as possible then you will need to have the right accessories. Like the chef, who cannot prepare a meal without the right tools, the grill expert should have an array of tools that will enable him or her to perform various tasks in grilling effectively and safely. Here's a closer look at the essential tools and accessories that will enhance your grilling adventures.

Meat Thermometer: In grilling and smoking, accuracy is crucial, and nothing is more valuable than a good quality instant-read meat thermometer. No matter if you have a piece of thick steak, the whole chicken, or flaky fish fillet, a meat thermometer guarantees that the food is perfectly cooked inside. This tool saves you the inconvenience of guessing and makes sure that whether you are cooking a steak, a chicken breast, or even ground beef, it is always tender and juicy but well-done.

Grill Tongs and Spatula: Working with foods on the grill calls for big utensils with long handles to prevent you from getting too close to the heat. Grill tongs are used to turn or move food around on the grill and a spatula is used to lift items and turn them such as fish and burgers. When selecting the tools for the grill, ensure that they have good grips and heatproof handles to enhance your grilling process.

Basting Brush: A basting brush is particularly useful when you need to apply marinades, sauces, or glazes on your food as it cooks. It assists you in applying flavors and at the same time, it helps in ensuring that your meats are well tenderized and juicy. Silicone brushes are especially useful because they can be used with high temperatures and are easy to clean.

Grill Cover: Most people invest a lot in grills, and thus it is important to ensure that your Traeger Grill is protected when not in use, and a good grill cover will ensure that it is protected from harsh weather conditions. It will also protect the grill from the harsh elements such as rain, snow, dust, and sun which may reduce the functionality of the grill and its lifespan.

Pellet Storage: Wood pellets are the fuel that runs the Traeger Grill, or more aptly, are the fuel that produces the heat and smoke that gives the food its flavor. Another critical factor is storage of the pellets to ensure that the pellets do not get wet since this is likely to lead to their deterioration. Storing and handling of these pellets requires airtight containers appropriate for the purpose of fuel storage and to retain the quality of the pellets.

Grill Brush: Grill cleaning after each use is a crucial step in ensuring the grill works well and does not cause fire accidents. A strong grill brush with brass or stainless-steel bristles will assist you in cleaning the grates of the BBQ and removing any food particles or grease that may have been left behind, this will help in preparing the BBQ for the next grilling process. It is also important to clean the grill regularly to avoid accumulation of dangerous bacteria and to improve the taste of the food.

Heat-Resistant Gloves: Shielding is needed when dealing with hot grates, pans and food on the grill. Heat-resistant gloves are designed to come between your hands and hot objects so that you can handle things without getting your hands burnt. These are helpful when trying to adjust the vents, refill the wood pellet, or to move the food around the grill.

Drip Pans and Foil Liners: Drip pans and foil liners help contain grease and spills, making it easier to clean up and minimizing flare-ups due to burning fats. These accessories assist in cleaning the interior of your grill and in preventing grease fire which makes it safer to grill.

Smoke Tubes and Boxes: To enhance the smoky flavor to your food, smoke tubes and boxes are good options to consider. These accessories enable you to put more wood pellets or chips, which gives off more smoke and better taste to the meals you are preparing.

Grill Mats and Baskets: Grill mats and baskets are ideal for preparing foods that are small or tender since they would easily slide through the bars. They also facilitate flipping and removal of food and assist in ensuring that the structure of meals is retained. Introducing these tools and accessories in your grilling station will not only improve the grilling and smoking but also make it an enjoyable and fast process.

1.3 Safety Tips and Best Practices

It is therefore important to follow some guidelines when grilling on your Traeger Grill to enjoy the best grilling process. Below are some of the important safety measures that should be taken and some of the safety precautions that should be observed to reduce the risks and enjoy barbeque grilling. Here is a closer look at how to grill safely: Before using the Traeger Grill, read through the product manual and safety guidelines that come with it. The first thing to do is to learn how to use the grill, and how to do so safely to avoid accidents and injuries. Grill maintenance and cleaning should be done routinely to enhance its durability, avoid flare-up and Grease fire.

Clean the grates, drip tray, and other surfaces that harbor food particles and grease after each use. Also, it is recommended to check the trap and clean it from grease build up to avoid blockage and clogging.

Grilling should always be done in an open space preferably out of the house to avoid accumulation of smoke. It is advisable not to grill in an enclosed area or near combustible materials such as dry leaves, branches, or wooden furniture. Proper ventilation ensures that smoke does not accumulate and that hazardous gases are not formed within the store. Grill safety tip: Never let your grill be out of sight while it is on. Stay attentive and be ready to add something if needed or turn the heat down if the food is burning. They can start at any one time, particularly when grilling fatty foods, so be alert and prepared to lower or turn the food or reduce the flame as required. One should ensure that when handling hot grates, hot pans or hot foods, one should use utensils and protective wears. Long-handled tongs, spatulas and heat resistant gloves are crucial to the safe handling of food on the grill and shielding the hands from burns. Do not use utensils with plastic handles as they may melt or even start a fire when placed in hot water.

When using gas in your Traeger Grill, ensure that you check for any leaks before each use of the grill. Wash the connections and hoses with a solution of soap and water, then ignite the gas. If the bubbles appear, it means that there is leakage, and you should not light the grill until you have solved the problem and turned off the supply of the gas. A barbecue can be an entertaining experience for the whole family, but it is vital to clear a safety circle around the grill and avoid letting children and pets near the grill area. Grilling can be dangerous because the high temperature can lead to burns, and touching the grill or other hot objects and flames are possible. Children should be closely monitored and kept away from the grilling area as well as pets when grilling.

1.4 Understanding Your Traeger Grill

What we have here is a completely different way of grilling that me and smoldering of wood pellets. A Traeger Grill grilling is exceptional to the conventional charcoal or gasoline grill since it relies on wood pellets as a fueling source, these are hardwood sawdust compressed together. These pellets are transported to a firepot through an auger feed system Then they are burned to release heat and smoke. One of the primary benefits of grill with wood pellet is that it can provide a steady heat and deliver a constant and robust flavored smoke. This consistency makes it easier to control heat when preparing the foods to ensure they are well cooked with that precious smoky flavor. Moving on to the features of the grill, the digital controller will allow you to regulate the temperature of the grill without having to guess or estimate the time required to cook your food.

Choosing the right wood pellets forms the important process of determining your grills efficiency and flavor output of your grilled foods. Wood pellets are the source of fuel for your grill, and the physical properties of this fuel determine the flavor, fragrance, and the quality of the food that is prepared on it. Knowing more about the wood pellets' features, advantages, and what kind of food is perfect for which type of wood will improve your grilling.

Wood pellet is biomass in the form of small, compressed hardwood saw dust and come in many types of wood providing the base type of smoke flavor. Popular hardwoods used are Hickory, Apple, Cherry, Mesquite, Oak, and Maple, among others. Wood pellets can therefore be regarded as having the following properties: The choice of the wood pellets must be influenced by the type of food you intend to prepare and the kind of taste you want to impress on your food.

Pellet types: Hickory pellets stand as one of the most preferred kinds as their well-defined smoky sweetness is perfectly balanced. It is good for all kinds of red meat like beef, pork and great for barbequing items such as ribs, briskets and pulled pork. Thick haze obtained by hickory pellets does not surrender to these tastes of meats and at the same time, it does not dominate it either.

This type of small sized Apple wood pellets has a mild and sweet flavoring that is best used for all types of poultry, pork, and baked products. Subtle peach and apricot flavors make it especially suitable for dishes based on poultry: chicken, turkey, and pork; the fruitiness contributes sweetness rather than becoming the focus for the dish. They can also be used in smoking of cheeses and vegetables, which makes them a good selection of apple pellets.

For instance, cherry wood pellets emit a slight taste of sweetness and fruits, and the taste accentuates the flavor of meats and vegetables adequately. They have subtle smoke from the cherry wood, and it can be utilized for almost any type of meat – chicken, pork, beef, lamb, etc. Furthermore, cherry pellets give the pork meat a reddish hue; this makes them popular with people who like to get an aesthetic value for their money.

The Mesquite pellets are excellent for their heavier and intense flavor which is suitable for grilling major cuts of meat such as steaks. The strong smoke produced by mesquite may be too intense in flavor if applied for longer months of smoking; therefore, it is ideal for short durations of smoking, and for meat varieties that do not require a long smoking process. In fact, this tree is used primarily in Texas-style barbecue and its taste is much appreciated in this dish.

Oak pellets are mid-range in smoke smells and do not have an overpowering flavor. They are an excellent option that could encompass brands of proteins like beef, pork, birds, and fish. Oak pellets produce a solid smoke taste that accentuates the distinctive taste or the food without masking it with a powerful smoky flavor, making them great for amateur and professional food preparation enthusiasts.

Maple pellets are crafted from the syrup of the maple tree and emit a gentle smoke that has a hint of sweetness making them ideal for poultry, pork, and vegetables. Encouraging The Right Kind of Smoke: Maple smoke gives it a subtle amount of sweetness that enhances the flavors of the food. Maple pellets also work well in smoking of cheeses because it gives a subtle smoke flavoring without over domination.

Some of the factors to consider when choosing the wood pellets include: the quality of the supply as well as its origin. As for the quality of the pellets, it is extraordinary: there are no additives, binders, or fillers in the production of the high-quality pellets, only 100% hardwood. These two are made of 100% wood which you will find gives you a cleaner smoke ring to the food and a better performance than the others. Moreover, other relevant recommendations that should be followed include proper storage of the pellets whereby they should be kept under a dry atmosphere because they may be affected due to the moisture which will reduce their efficiency when burnt. Moreover, you can also try different kinds of pellet blends, other than the type of wood that is used for the production of pellets. Most brand envision various degrees of merging specific wood types to express variability in taste. For instance, hickory and applewood are good together for they bring out a very strong smoke with a touch of sweetness that can complement different types of meat.

1.6 Basic Grill Maintenance, Care and Troubleshooting Common Issues

There are some recommended procedures which when followed to the letter will make the smoker lengthy lasting productive and constantly put out tasteful smokey results. Besides, what many people fail to understand is maintaining your grill is very important not only makes your grill run smoothly but also have the guarantee that the food you cook over it is perfectly cooked. You don't need to spend a lot of money in expensive services just to clean and maintain your grill, you can do it yourself here are the steps to follow:

To maintain your grill, cleaning is the most important factor one needs to embrace daily or at least occasionally. Some easy-to-follow tips are listed as follows: always let the grill cool before you begin the cleaning process after you are done using it. Starting with the fact, to clean the interior of the grill, you will need to rid the grates of any food deposits with a brush that features rigid bristles. This is because when the matrix ignites the next time, it burns particles of food stuck on the surface, leaving unwanted flavors in your food. of course, it also helps to keep your barbecue grates free of stickiness and already for your next round of grilling. The next thing that ought to be checked is the drip tray and the hamburgers grease management system and they have to be cleansed. However, the grills usually collect grease and drippings as time passes which can cause fires, in addition to compromising on performance. Empty the drip tray and greasing bucket and get rid of the accumulated grease in the they correctly. To clean the drip tray, use warm water with soap ensure that you use a sponge that is nonabrasive to avoid scratching the surface. For more stubborn grease deposits, one may be required to apply a grill cleaner for efficient removal of the grease layers. Before re-installing the drip tray, it is important that scraps of food and water are washed off and dried, respectively.

Plying a Traeger grill comes with the routine responsibility of desisting the inside of your grill from ash and pellet dust buildup. First, remove any ash that may have accumulated at the bottom of the fire pot as it acts as a barrier that may hamper the flow of air towards the fuel. When cleaning acrylic nails, it is most effective to use a shop vacuum or a handheld vacuum that features a hose attachment. Furthermore, make sure that the interior walls of the grill and its base should also be clean from ash and grease: you can use a sponge soaked in warm water to clean the interior of the BBQ grill.

The hopper is the compartment where you put your wood pellets, and it always requires maintenance to ensure proper pellet supply with no interferences like debris. Sometimes, the hopper should be emp t and cleaned for dust or left-over pellet residues. To do this, one should use a vacuum to remove every particle of dust that may be found on it, to ensure that the mechanism of an auger must be free for moving of the pellets. In the case of wood pellet stoves, moisture is the biggest abuse that you can give to your pellets, so ensure that the hopper is dry before you put the new batch of pellets in it.

The auger is an essential part of the barbeque, as it oversees moving the pellets from the hopper to the firepot. Some common auger problems include belt hopper and feeder along with variations in heat and smoke, which can be solved by conducting a proper and frequent inspection and servicing of auger. From the control panel, locate the section that checks on the auger for any forms of blockage or instances of jamming involving the pellets. If you still find problems, you should take apart the auger as per the various directions provided by the company, remove the blockage, and then reinstall it. Regular greasing of the auger mechanism is also a good idea that would enable one to avoid any hitch.

The storage and protection of your grill are significant factors that can help in avoiding the need for frequent replacement. Regularly store your grill in a sheltered area, or when they are not in use, cover with a water-resistant grill cover. This is particularly crucial if your grill is used and stored outdoors, given that adverse weather conditions can result to formation of rust as well as corrosion. It is important to make sure that the grill is cool to touch before putting the cover on in order not to cause damage on the cover due to heat. In case you live in a region with cold weather, or you decided to experience the pleasures of grilling only in warmer months it's better to store your grill in a garage or a shed. Before storing, clean the part and ensure that the hopper is free from pellets to avoid any chance of absorbing moisture and thus forming mold. Turn off the grill and cover it to safely prevent any kind of accident from occurring.

It would be useful to clean and inspect the equipment more thoroughly at least once a year. This means removing some of the parts such as the grates, the drip tray, the heat baffle, and the fire pot and ensure that they are cleaned.

This involves removing parts such as the grate, the drip tray, the heat baffle, and fire pot for cleaning. Check for any sign of usage that might affect the quality of the grill such as rust or other signs of breakage. It is advisable to check for any loose screws or bolts and if you find any, then to tighten them. Having a check-up annually would ensure that your grill is well maintained and ready to go for another year of the grilling fun.

Nevertheless, there are few problems that many Traeger Grill users face even if it's built with resilience qualities. Research on typical failures and how to deal with them can also assist you in diagnosing issues. If the grill is not getting hot enough, check cleaner for the clogged auger and make sure firepot is not dirty. There are two things that may cause the grill shut off; the power drop or the hopper is empty. c) The hopper should always be full of the pellets; remember to check the power connections. In this case check whether the grill is placed on a flat surface and the heat baffle is well placed on the surface of the fixture. Simple maintenance practices and frequent repair works will go a notch higher in guaranteeing a perfect grill experience throughout the service period.

1.7 Mastering Grilling Techniques

A great summary of the topic of grilling skills is an important make or break aspect to successful grilling. Hence, with your Traeger Grill, you are a chef on call with a functional, full-range barbeque equipment whose functions includes direct and indirect grilling, searing, and smoking. This chapter will enable you get acquainted with some of the basic intermediaries that make a chef to get flawless output every time.

Direct vs. Indirect Grilling

For one to master the difference between direct and Indirect grilling it very important especially when handling different types of foods to enhance the cooking process.

Barbecuing is done by placing the food right on the heat source while using low-intensity heat with long cooking times. This method is the best used on food items that don't take long to cook, in instances like steaks, burgers, hot dogs, and vegetables. The fats from the direct grilling authority tenderize the outside of the food and make it crisp while keeping it moist on the inside. To give some recommendations on direct grilling on your Traeger, it is always recommended that you set your Traeger to high and put foods directly on the grill grates over the heat.

They include direct and indirect grilling; while in direct grilling, foods are arranged directly above the heat source, indirect grilling takes place on the other side. It is ideal where large, thick cuts of meats, which will take a long time to cook thoroughly are involved such as whole chickens, turkeys, and ribs, among others. The heat is not directly placed on the food but is used to heat up the surroundings and so the food takes more time to cook, and the inside part becomes soft while the outer part is not burnt. For indirect grilling, on your Traeger you put the food you want to cook on one side of the grill and the heat is on the other side, or you use the heat baffle or deflector to create a convection grilling.

Searing Techniques

Caramelization is a browning technique that involves the use of heat to form a browned layer on the outside layer of the food without compromising the internal texture of the food product. For conventional surface browning, for high heat searing preheat the grill to the highest level which is normally 450-500 degrees Fahrenheit. When the grill is ready, it is time to put the meat on the grill and get its surface perfectly seared on both sides which usually takes 3-5 minutes depending on the amount of meat and the power of the heat. This way is good for all types of steaks, chops, and some specific types of vegetables.

Searing is not possible on all Traeger models due to the general inability to crank up the heat beyond 450 or 500°F, though some newer Traeger models feature a separate searing broiler or a grill surface attachment that enables instant searing opportunities. Some of them can heat to much higher than the flat surface of the grill, and this makes it possible to achieve the desired sear level. Presumably, warm the sear station, and utilize it to succulent sear something at a high temperature rapidly, preceding moving it to the much cooler indirect grilling zone. Another good method of searing involves using a cast iron skillet or griddle on your Traeger. Place your skillet onto the grill then heat it until becomes so hot, with smoke coming out of it, and the last step is you put your meat into the hot skillet. Nonetheless, the material used in the construction of this cast iron grill makes it retain heat for long and is very effective in sealing foods to grill for a perfect meal. Seems very helpful especially for pieces of scallops or vegetables as those more tender foods need fast, subjecting them to evenly heated sear.

Reverse searing can be effectively described as the process of cooking in both low heat and high heat or as the combination of slow and fast cooking because it follows the two processes. This technique can be extremely beneficial in cook "thick" cuts is the best word to describe this technique is helpful when cooking meat cuts like the ribeye or tomahawk steaks and ends in providing an excellent crust on the exterior. Here's the step-by-step reverse searing. Here's the step-by-step reverse searing:

Slow Cook First: Start browning the skin side of the meat over high heat and then move it to a cooler part of the grill and cook the meat slowly at a low temperature of about 225-250°F until it reaches an internal temperature of around 5-10 degrees below where they like it. This slow cooking phase helps the meat come to the required temperature and get cooked from all sides and angles without getting a crust on its surface.

Rest and Preheat: After getting your meat to the optimal temperature range, transfer it off the grill to let it sit as you bring the grill to the 450-500°F range for the charbroil step.

Sear: Once the grill is hot, you need to return the meat to the grill where it will be positioned right over the hot area. Grill each side for 1-2 minutes until it gets a nice brown color or charred. The meat should now be ready: the outside nicely browned all over, while the insides tender and succulent.

Reverse searing allows the meat to be cooked at a lower temperature over a longer period, thus avoiding a situation where one side ends up burnt while the other is not well done, while also giving the finished product an exceptional tenderness and taste. Proper airflow is required to be established to ensure that the selected level of smoke is complemented. Make sure that the vent of the grill is properly opened set by a good amount of space so that air can circulate properly. If there is little airflow, the fuel does not combust thoroughly, leading to bitter smoke P11 The smoke would go up quickly if there is too much airflow. It will also help to get optimum results without over-cooking or making the food too smoky that will change its taste when the smoke flavor is being added.

Learning these main grilling strategies and further grilling mastery about the right direct grilling and indirect grilling, searing, and smoke options, you will be on the right side of the path to grilling mastery. All these methods have their uses and can allow you to get a huge variety of tastes and consistencies while cooking on the Traeger Grill, which makes your experiments in culinary field both interesting and stimulating.

Chapter 2: Breakfast on the Grill

Good morning, grill enthusiasts! Imagine waking up to the smell of sizzling bacon wafting through the air, accompanied by the comforting warmth of freshly grilled pancakes. Welcome to the world of breakfast on the grill, where mornings become extraordinary. This chapter is all about transforming your breakfast routine into a flavorful adventure. Whether you're a fan of the classic bacon and eggs or eager to try something new like smoked cinnamon rolls, we've got you covered.

Using your Traeger Grill, you'll discover how to infuse your morning favorites with smoky goodness, creating meals that are as delightful as they are memorable. Picture grilling breakfast burritos stuffed with savory sausage and hash browns, or preparing a smoked breakfast casserole that brings everyone to the table. Each recipe is designed to start your day with a burst of flavor and a touch of grill mastery. So, grab your coffee, fire up your Traeger, and let's make breakfast the best part of your day.

2.1 Smoked Bacon and Eggs

Serves: 4

Cooking Time: 30 minutes

Temperature: 375°F

Simply prepare smoked bacon and eggs to be cooked on the grate of your Traeger grill and this will indeed be a breakfast to remember. The bacon's smoky taste and complimented the yolk of the eggs when they were done, giving those individuals a mouthwatering and fulfilling meal in the morning. As you can notice, this dish is created with the help of few components, and all you need is your Traeger and several hours.

Ingredients:

> - 8 slices thick-cut bacon
> - 8 large eggs
> - Salt and pepper to taste
> - Fresh parsley, chopped (for garnish)

Instructions:

- Begin by initializing the Traeger grill for cooking at 375 degrees Fahrenheit. Close the lid and allow it to come up to temperature while you prepare the bacon and eggs.

- Place the bacon slices directly on the bars of the grill immediately and ensure that they are arranged to have ample space between them. Lift the top and let the bacon smoke for fifteen minutes or until it reaches brown softness on the surfaces.

- As the bacon cooks share a heavy smoke add the eggs to a separate bowl and proceed to beat them and add salt and pepper to enhance the flavor. This cuisine requires beating eggs until the yolks and whites are thoroughly mixed.'

- After the bacon has started to sizzle on the Traeger, one should be very careful when pulling out the grill grate with the bacon out of the grill. Pour it directly on the grill grate starting from the center, ensuring that it covers the whole surface to create an even layer.

- Put back the grill grate on the Traeger and close the lid if there is still sufficient charcoal left. Leave the bacon and eggs to cook for another 10-15 minutes or until the eggs are well done and the bacon is hyper crispy.

- After achieving the desired consistency of eggs and crispiness of bacon, use aggravated grasps to remove the grill grate off the Traeger. Using a spatula, the yummy bacon and eggs that were prepared should then be moved to the serving plates. Complete the eggs with chopped fresh parsley to add flavor and color to your meal.

- Smoked bacon and eggs can be served hot and accompanied with any best-known breakfast garnishes like toast, hash browns, or fruits. Wash it down, enjoy the BBQ like flavors of this mouthwatering brekky delight.

Tips:

- For a fancier product, he said shredded cheese could be added on top of the eggs a few minutes before the end of cooking time.

- You can omit or change any of these ingredients to your desired choice, such as chopped green onions, thyme, or smokey sweet paprika.

- They do recommend you add the eggs to the grill and cook the bacon for a few minutes longer than the above video demonstrates.

- Don't forget to keep an eye on the grill temperature to ensure even cooking and prevent any burning or overcooking.

2.2 Grilled French Toast

Serves: 4

Cooking Time: 20 minutes

Temperature: 350°F

Grilled French toast is a very rich item and is a variation on one of the most traditional breakfast meals. Grilling it on the Traeger Grill enhances the sea boiled flavor and transforms this dish to another level. This is a dish with a crispy golden-brown crust and soft inside, creating a delicious grilled French toast that will become one of your favorite brunch meals.

Ingredients:

- ➢ 8 slices thick-cut bread (such as brioche or challah)
- ➢ 4 large eggs
- ➢ 1 cup milk
- ➢ 2 tablespoons granulated sugar
- ➢ 1 teaspoon vanilla extract
- ➢ 1/2 teaspoon ground cinnamon
- ➢ Butter or cooking spray, for greasing the grill

Instructions:

- Begin by setting your Traeger Grill to 175°C for the first stage, and then increase to 200°C when you are ready for the final cooking. Pull the lid down and let the griddle heat up while you mix the French toast ingredients in a bowl.

- These are the steps of preparing the ingredients and mixture, in a dish or a bowl combine the eggs, milk, sugar the vanilla extract and cinnamon. This will be your French toast batter Make sure to whisk the eggs and the milk to make a smooth batter.

- Ladle the French toast batter on both sides of each bread slice to ensure that it is well-saturated. Some of the oil will float on the surface of the batter: wipe it off with absorbent paper, then turn the bread out on to a plate.

- Before putting food directly on the grill grates season the grates with butter or a cooking spray. After the bread is soaked, arrange it on the grill grates without using any tongs or flipping it around.

- Lastly, cover the pan with its lid and allow the French toast to cook for, 5-7 minutes on each side until nicely browned and crispy on the surface and ashen on the interior.

- After the French toast has been grilled to the stage that suits your taste, take it out of the cooking process and place it on plates. Enjoy with warm and you can add some toppings like maple syrup, fresh fruits, powered sugar, whipped cream, and others.

- Go and try it, feel the fun and the savoriness of your grilled French toast. This is one of those dishes ideal for that wonderful, relaxed morning breakfast or any breakfast time when you feel like indulging in something delicious and easy on the system.

Tips:

- To add more taste, it is recommended to use flavored bread like cinnamon bread or ideally raisin bread.

- Spoon the batter onto the bread and flip the bread over and put it on the hot pan You may add toppings to the French toast such as sliced bananas, chopped nuts, chocolate sauce or any of your preferred toppings.

- However, if you prefer your bread to be a little softer you could allow it to absorb more batter by soaking it before grilling it on the grill.

- Do not crowd the grill grates it is recommended that you arrange them in a manner that provides enough space between them, meaning you should not pack them tightly. If you require to cook the French toast for a group, then arrange the pieces in batches to fry so that they do not stick together.

2.3 Smoked Sausage and Hash Browns

Serves: 4

Cooking Time: 30 minutes

Temperature: 375°F

It is a delicious and easy-to-cook meal that can directly be served during breakfast, for example, smoked sausage and hash browns. Smoked Sausage Hash Browns is a delicious recipe that is perfect for breakfast as it has the potential of providing you with the energy you require to carry out your daily tasks.

Ingredients:

- ➢ 1 pound smoked sausage, sliced
- ➢ 4 cups frozen hash browns
- ➢ 1 onion, diced
- ➢ 1 bell pepper, diced
- ➢ 2 cloves garlic, minced
- ➢ Salt and pepper to taste
- ➢ Olive oil
- ➢ Fresh parsley, chopped (for garnish)

Instructions:

- First, turn your Traeger Grill up to the recommended temperature setting of 375°F and wait for the appliance to heat up to the right temperature.

- For the meat to cook uniformly on the grill, particularly on the FAT side, I prepare when the grill is initially turned on. Prepare for assembling, they also want to slice the smoked sausage into rounds, chop the onion and bell pepper, and the garlic should be minced.

- Place the skillet [or your cast-iron pan] on the grill and heat it up, then add olive oil into the pan. To begin with, in the same pan put the sliced smoked sausage and fry until they are brown both at the surface and at the middle for about 5-7minutes. After that, take off the sausage from the pan and put in another place.

- If you need more olive oil repeat the process of sautéing the vegetables by adding olive oil into the same skillet or pan. To this add diced onion and bell pepper and cook for a few minutes until they give up their crunch, around 3-4 minutes. Sauté garlic and once it turns slightly brown, add in the mushrooms, and cook for one minute longer.

- Mix the cooked vegetables with the frozen hash browns you set aside earlier. Arrange them in a single layer and then leave them to roast for some time without getting upset so that they become crispy from the bottom side.

- Once they have begun to turn brown, return the cooked sausage back to the pan. Mix everything as one now and continue to cook until the hash browns are golden brown and crispy, and sausage is hot.

- Season the smoked sausage and hash browns using lightly sea salt and black pepper. Sprinkle minced fresh parsley over the top of the recipe for color and added flavor.

- Spoon the smoked sausage and hash browns to a serving dish or make individual dishes out of them. Serve hot and enjoy!

Tips:

- If preferred, the recipe outlined here could also contain other vegetables such as mushrooms, spinach, or cherry tomatoes.

- You can also include the shredded cheese on top of the hash browns towards the end of cooking time for a nice brown and cheesy topping.

- As any traditional breakfast dishes, this dish would be best served accompanied by ketchup, hot sauce, or salsa.

- For those with a taste for something hotter, you could use spicy smoked sausage or even provide red pepper flakes to sprinkle on the hash browns.

2.4 Grilled Breakfast Burritos

Serves: 4

Cooking Time: 20 minutes

Temperature: 375°F

Grilled breakfast burritos are yummy and can effectively fulfill the nutritional needs of persons in the morning.
Grilled breakfast burritos are a delicious and convenient way to enjoy a hearty morning meal. Filled with eggs, cheese, your choice of breakfast meat and any other thing you fancy, these burritos are perfect and easy to prepare for individuals on the move. Preparing them on your grill gives them an extra special barbecue flavor that

makes them sublime.

Ingredients:

- ➢ 8 large eggs
- ➢ 1/4 cup milk
- ➢ Salt and pepper to taste
- ➢ 1 tablespoon olive oil
- ➢ 1/2 pound breakfast sausage, cooked and crumbled
- ➢ 1 cup shredded cheddar cheese
- ➢ 1 cup diced bell peppers
- ➢ 1/2 cup diced onions
- ➢ 4 large flour tortillas
- ➢ Salsa, sour cream, avocado, for serving (optional)

Instructions:

- You should heat your Traeger Grill to medium-high heat, which is about 375°F and wait until it comes to the proper cooking temperature.

- Add the eggs, milk, salt, and pepper to a bowl and whisk them until well combined for the next procedure. Turn on the grill and fry a skillet or cast-iron pan and pour the olive oil. Pour the egg mixture from the bowl into the pan and continue frying until it reaches a desired stage of cooking. To prepare the dish take the following steps: Put water and rice together and cook. Pour melted butter into meat mixture and stir well.

- Spread the flour tortillas on the clean area of the counter or any flat and clean hard surface. Sprinkle the cooked scrambled eggs, crumbled breakfast sausage, shredded cheddar cheese, diced bell peppers and onions over them in a single layer so they are distributing evenly on the tortillas.

- Pull up the bottom of each tortilla on opposite sides of the filling and tuck them over the filling and then roll up the tortilla with the filling from the bottom.

- After you have stacked the burritos arrange them directly over the grill minimizing contact with the grate with the seam down. After that, close the lid and grill the tortillas for about 5 minutes on each side depending on the color that you want, either crispy golden brown or soft with grill imprint on it.

- When cooked, take out the grilled breakfast burritos from the grill and place on plating bowls. Be ready to accompany with such garnishing as salsa, sour cream or avocado.

Tips:

- Court the breakfast burritos to your preference; a plate of diced tomatoes, black beans, cooked bacon, diced ham, among others.

- If you want to have vegetarian Sausage or Tofu scramble, exclude the breakfast sausage.

- This can be done before barbecuing or baking the burritos so that they will be easier to turn on the grill as well as avoiding any filling from spilling out.

- The fun thing about these is that they can be assembled a day or two before and then reheated in the morning, so you don't have to worry about a time-consuming breakfast through the weekdays.

2.5 Grilled Bagels with Smoked Salmon

Serves: 4

Cooking Time: 15 minutes

Temperature: 375°F

Smoked salmon bagel is crustacean and breakfast or brunch dish that is equally easy to cook on Traeger grill. In combination with the smoky taste of the grill, the product tastes exquisite due to the saltiness of smoked fish.

Ingredients:

- 4 bagels, sliced in half
- 8 ounces smoked salmon
- 4 ounces cream cheese, softened
- 1 tablespoon capers
- 1/4 red onion, thinly sliced
- Fresh dill, for garnish

Instructions:

- Setting up the grill to active super-heat mode, bring the heat of the Traeger Grill to 375 degrees F. Let it sit until it boils, centered over the stove while you go through the process of preparing the bagels.

- Position the basted bagel slice directly on the grill grates of your Traeger without interference. Shut the lid and grill for 3 to 4 minutes, or until yes, the bread is slightly toasted.

- Top the toasted bagel half with a thin coat of softened cream cheese. Place top slices of smoked salmon, thin strip of raw red onion and capers on it.

- Presenting before you the recipe of Grilled Bagels with Cream Cheese and Smoked salmon: Finally, garnish the grilled bagels with the fresh dill sprigs. Serve immediately and enjoy!

Tips:

- o Use of condiments such as lemon juice or black pepper, especially to the assembled bagels, will give the bread a tastier feel.

- o You can add other toppings of your preference or include other garnishes such as sliced cucumber, avocado or tomato.

- o Accompany these bagels grilled to perfection with smoked salmon and some fresh fruits or wash them down with a green salad for a delicious and healthy meal.

2.6 Grilled Avocado Toast

Serves: 4

Cooking Time: 10 minutes

Temperature: 375°F

Grilled avocado toast is different and flavorful with melted cheese, crispy toast, and delicious toppings that are roasted and infused with the Traeger grill smoky flavor. Ideal for a quick snack, or even for the first meal of the day, breakfast or for a light meal that still serves as a lunch, this is all that everybody may need.

Ingredients:

- ➢ 2 ripe avocados

- ➤ 4 slices of your favorite bread (such as sourdough or whole grain)
- ➤ 2 tablespoons olive oil
- ➤ Salt and pepper to taste
- ➤ Optional toppings: sliced tomatoes, crumbled feta cheese, red pepper flakes, microgreens

Instructions:

- Start off by preheating your Traeger Grill to moderate heat of about 375 degrees Fahrenheit. Let it warm, as you prepare the avocados and breads to be toasted.

- First, slice the avocados through their equators and then separate the pit from the flesh of each avocado. Take the avocado flesh and place it in a bowl, and then you should proceed to mash it until there are no lumps left. Do this to season with salt and pepper to the preferred amount of taste.

- On each slice of bread make sure to put olive oil on both the sides. Lay the slices of bread directly on the grates of your Traeger and cook for 3 to 4 min on one side and 3 to 4 on the other or until the bread turns golden brown and crispy.

- For this recipe, one needs to spread a substantial layer of mashed avocado on each of the grilled bread slices. Finish off the dish with additional preferred garnishes like diced tomatoes, crumbled feta cheese, chili flakes, or microgreens.

- Serve the grilled avocado toast while it is hot to maximize the enjoyment of eating the dish. Dig into the rich creamy avocado, crunchy bread alongside the delicious toppings of your choice, all of which get a flavor boost when grilled on a Traeger Grill.

Tips:

- You can play around with different toppings to accommodate the preferences of your personal palate.

- Simply chop it and put it on top of avocado toast, serve with a poached or fried egg for extra protein.

- Pour balsamic glazed or hot sauce over them for added taste.

2.7 Smoked Breakfast Casserole

Serves: 6

Cooking Time: 1 hour

Temperature: 350°F

Smoked breakfast casserole consists of the ingredients that are traditionally used in the preparation of casserole and is a delicious hearty breakfast meal for large groups. This casserole recipe which included eggs, cheese, breakfast meat and vegetables are simple to prepare but full of taste.

Ingredients:

- 8 large eggs
- 1 cup milk
- Salt and pepper to taste
- 1 pound breakfast sausage, cooked and crumbled
- 1 bell pepper, diced
- 1 onion, diced
- 2 cups shredded cheddar cheese
- 4 cups frozen hash browns, thawed
- Optional toppings: chopped green onions, sliced tomatoes, salsa

Instructions:

- Place the Switch Quadrant onto the Traeger Grill and preheat the Traeger Grill to 350°F. Let it warm up as you are organizing the ingredients for this casserole and preparing it.

- To make the batter, in a large mixing bowl, beat the eggs, milk, salt, and pepper together, making sure they are well incorporated. Add the cooked and crumbled breakfast sausage into the mixture, diced bell pepper, onion, cheddar cheese and thawed hash browns mixing everything until it's evenly incorporated.

- Next pour this egg mixture into a greased baking dish that measures 9×13 inches. Position the baking dish directly on the grates of the Traeger and smoke for 45-50 minutes up to the point to which the casserole has set and tops are golden brown.

- Pull the smoked breakfast casserole off the grill and then allow it to sit for at least five minutes prior to slicing. Optional garnishing can include green onions, tomatoes, or salsa in case of a preferred topping. Cut into desired sizes and best enjoyed when consumed while still hot.

Tips:

- o It's an awesome meal for the family and can be extended with a preferred vegetable or meat of your choice.

- o If you are using the vegetarian diet, then do not add breakfast sausage or replace it with vegetarian sausage or tofu, respectively.

- o Prepare the casserole and prepare it for smoking the night before, so the next morning, you are sure to get one of the tastiest smoky breakfasts you could ever imagine.

2.8 Grilled Pancakes

Serves: 4

Cooking Time: 15 minutes

Temperature: 375°F

Grilled pancakes are fun and creative spin on your traditional pancake which deeply enhance the flavor through the grilling process. You can prepare pancakes, and when doing so, the flavor of the Traeger grill is imparted on the food as well as the fluffiness increased.

Ingredients:

- ➢ 1 1/2 cups all-purpose flour
- ➢ 3 1/2 teaspoons baking powder
- ➢ 1 teaspoon salt
- ➢ 1 tablespoon granulated sugar
- ➢ 1 1/4 cups milk
- ➢ 1 large egg
- ➢ 3 tablespoons unsalted butter, melted
- ➢ Optional toppings: maple syrup, fresh berries, whipped cream

Instructions:

- Please select the grill of Traeger and set it to resolve 375°F before commencing the cooking session. Let it come to pressure while you fry the pancake.

- For the first step, combining the dry ingredients, mix the flour, baking powder, salt, and sugar together in a large sized bowl until they are well combined. In the second bowl, combine milk, egg, and the melted butter through the wholesome process of beating. This is done by first pouring the wet ingredients into the dry ingredients and mixing until you observe the flour mixture not fully combining with the wet ingredients. Do not be too vigorous or over mix the place as this will make the pancakes firm.

- This grill method needs the grill grates of your Traeger to be lightly greased with cooking spray or butter. To cook the pancakes, use a ladle or a cup and dip it into the batter to pour it over the hot grill creating circles of the preferred size. Cover the lid and fry for about 2-5 minutes on each side depending on the heat or until it turns brownish and really cooked.

- Finally, here are the detailed instructions on how to prepare the recipes: Remove the grilled pancakes from the grill and serve them immediately with your favorite toppings, such as maple syrup, fresh berries, or whipped cream. These grilled pancakes are perfect for those who love the flavors and the smokiness while the texture has been made softer.

Tips:

- Introduce alterations to the basic pancake solution, adding various ingredients such as chocolate chips, bananas, or nuts into the blend.

- You can always warm the rest of the pancakes in the oven since you will make more batches of them, just put them in a baking sheet and place the baking sheet in a low oven heat, around 200°F.

- It's best to serve these grilled pancakes with other breakfast meals that are on the spicy side such as bacon or sausage.

2.9 Smoked Frittata

Serves: 6

Cooking Time: 35 minutes

Temperature: 350°F

Smoked frittata is a tasty and easily consumable meal for different occasions, such as breakfast, brunch, or dinner. With eggs, cheese, and your favorite vegetables enclosed in its lightweight frame, this frittata is easy to create and delicious.

Ingredients:

- ➢ 8 large eggs
- ➢ 1/2 cup milk
- ➢ Salt and pepper to taste
- ➢ 1 tablespoon olive oil
- ➢ 1 onion, diced
- ➢ 1 bell pepper, diced
- ➢ 1 cup diced cooked ham or bacon
- ➢ 1 cup shredded cheese (such as cheddar or mozzarella)
- ➢ Optional toppings: chopped fresh herbs, sliced tomatoes

Instructions:

- Set your Traeger Grill between 350 and 325°F. Leave it to warm up for some time while you chop the ingredients needed to prepare the frittata.

- To prepare the batter, crack about 4 large eggs and whisk it together with ¼ cup milk, salt, and pepper in a large mixing bowl. Set aside. Prepare your grill for stovetop grilling, then add the olive oil in a cast iron skillet or a pan that can safely be taken in the oven.

- Add the diced onion and bell pepper should be added to the skillet where they should be cooked for about five minutes. Subsequently, incorporate the diced ham or bacon and incorporate gently for another 2-3 minutes, or until sizzling.

- Then pour the egg well combined mixture on the cooked vegetables and meat in the same skillet. Gently place mixture into cups and top with shredded cheese.

- Also, put the skillet directly on the grates of the pre-heated Traeger grill and then shut its lid. Bake the frittata in smoke for 25-30 minutes until the eggs are well-done and the surface of the frittata becomes golden brown color.

- After the frittata has been smoked, transfer it from the grill and let it to rest for few minutes before it is sliced. Optional: add more chopped fresh herbs and / or tomato slices. Prepare the squash by slicing the halves into wedges and serve as is preferably warm, but they are also good when served at room temperature.

Tips:

- You can spice up your smoked frittata with additional vegetables or even meats that you prefer.

- Adjust the heat gradually when cooking and remember to grease the skillet well before putting the eggs on it to avoid sticking.

- Refrigeration of the frittata: Since frittata can still be reheated, it can be preserved in the fridge for up to 3 days, and then warmed up in the microwave or the oven.

2.10 Grilled Breakfast Pizza

Serves: 6

Cooking Time: 20 minutes

Temperature: 400°F

In this case, the moments of the preparation and cooking of the grilled breakfast pizza are obvious and compelling. Served with eggs, cheese, breakfast sausage, and vegetables, this pizza is both hearty and delicious with a versatile build.

Ingredients:

- 1 pound pizza dough, homemade or store-bought
- 1/2 cup pizza sauce
- 1 cup shredded mozzarella cheese
- 4 large eggs
- 1/2 cup cooked and crumbled breakfast sausage
- 1/2 cup diced bell pepper
- 1/4 cup diced onion
- Salt and pepper to taste

- ➢ Optional toppings: sliced mushrooms, cooked bacon, sliced tomatoes, chopped fresh herbs

Instructions:

- Drain your Traeger Grill to 400°F before you start cooking. Let it heat up a little more while you are getting ready to put the pizza toppings on the dough.

- Pat the pizza dough on a lightly floured surface into the thin that you want. Move the rolled-out dough to a pizza peel or a baking sheet if it is one that is non-stick and covered with parchment paper.

- Next, spread the pizza sauce on the rolled-out dough to the right thickness while ensuring that you leave approximately 1 cm of space around the edges. Then pour the sauce over the lasagna and cover with the rest of the mozzarella cheddar cheese. Place the cheese on the base, and then put the cooked and crumbled breakfast sausage, diced bell pepper, and diced onion on top.

- Gently proceed to break the eggs on the pizza and distribute them well on the pile of toppings. From the prepared eggs, put the salt and pepper on them to your preferred percentage.

- Place the assembled pizza directly in the grill grates of your Traeger, then pull the lid over to lock it into place. This has to be done for about 15-20 minutes or until the crust turns a golden-brown color, and the eggs have solidified.

- Once the grilled breakfast pizza is ready, take it off the grill and allow it to sit for 5 to 10 minutes to reduce heat before slicing. For a delightful extra, top with any of the following: sauteed mushrooms; crisp bacon; sliced fresh tomatoes; or fresh herbs snipped into small pieces. You should cut pizza into pieces, and it is best served hot.

Tips:

- o For a crispy pizza crust, it is recommended that you grill the dough for up to 5-7 minutes before you add toppings onto your pizza.

- o You can easily add or remove any topping that you may not prefer or add any other toppings you want. Extra parts such as sliced mushrooms, cooked bacon, or even sliced tomatoes can as well be introduced into the recipe.

- o It is also important that the eggs should be placed in pizza at some equal intervals to make them to cook in equal interval.

- o Refrigerated pizza can be eaten the next day or even the following days if you consume it within 3 days After preparing your pizza, put the leftover pizza in a container and store it in the refrigerator to keep it fresh for the next day.

Chapter 3: Appetizers and Snacks

Who doesn't love a good appetizer or snack? Whether you're hosting a gathering, enjoying a casual weekend, or just need a tasty bite, appetizers and snacks are essential. This chapter is your ultimate guide to creating delicious, crowd-pleasing bites on your Traeger Grill.

Imagine serving a platter of smoked chicken wings with a perfectly balanced smoky and spicy kick or enjoying the gooey goodness of grilled nachos with melted cheese and your favorite toppings. From the zesty thrill of grilled jalapeño peppers to the comforting taste of smoked deviled eggs, each recipe is crafted to be easy, flavorful, and sure to impress.

We've included a variety of options to suit every palate and occasion. You'll find everything from finger foods that are perfect for game day to sophisticated bites for your next dinner party. So, let's get grilling and turn every snack time into a celebration of flavor.

3.1 Smoked Chicken Wings

Serves: 6

Cooking Time: 1 hour

Temperature: 325° (smoke) then 375°

In many cultures, especially in America, Smoke chicken wings is popular snack food that typically served before the main dish and is commonly prepared during occasions such as game day. This is because when you cook them slow on your Traeger Grill the smoke penetrates deep into the flayers thus giving the wings that juicy textured feel.

Ingredients:

> ➤ 3 pounds chicken wings
> ➤ 2 tablespoons olive oil
> ➤ 2 tablespoons barbecue rub or seasoning of your choice
> ➤ Barbecue sauce for serving (optional)
> ➤ Celery sticks and ranch or blue cheese dressing for dipping

Instructions:

- To smoke the ribs, start the Traeger Grill at 225°F. Let it sit undisturbed while you arrange the chicken wings as per your planned preparation.

- Removing moisture: Drain/ pat the chicken wings dry with paper towels to remove any moisture that may be on the skin. Place during wings in a bowl and then coat with olive oil and barbecue rub to achieve an even distribution.

- Superimpose the seasoned chicken wings on the grill grate of your Traeger specifically. Bolt the lid and smoke for 30-40 minutes, or until you are certain that the wings have developed a sufficient level of smokiness.

- You should raise the temperature of your Traeger Grill to 375 degrees Fahrenheit for the third and last method of cooking.

- After that, leave the chicken wings to grill at the higher temperature for about 20-30 minutes until they are of brown color and thoroughly cooked with crispy skin on the outside.

- Take smoked chicken wings out of the allotted grill and let them sit for a few minutes before consuming. If desired, you may also baste them lightly with the barbecue sauce before grilled. Enjoy it hot preferably with celery sticks and dipping in ranch or blue cheese.

Tips:

- For extra crispy wings, you can finish them under a broiler for a few minutes after smoking.

- Try out various barbecue rubs or seasonings to your desire as to achieve the different tenderness of wings.

- Serve these smoked chicken wings as an appetizer or main dish alongside other game day favorites like nachos or sliders.

3.2 Grilled Jalapeño Poppers

Serves: 8

Cooking Time: 45 minutes

Temperature: 375°F

Grilled jalapeño peppers are very spicy as well as flavorful, which makes it the best appetizer for any occasion including parties and barbecues. Stuffed peppers – The cream cheese stuffed peppers are wrapped in bacon and cooked on your Traeger Grill.

Ingredients:

- ➢ 16 large jalapeño peppers
- ➢ 8 ounces cream cheese, softened
- ➢ 1 cup shredded cheddar cheese
- ➢ 1 teaspoon garlic powder
- ➢ 1/2 teaspoon smoked paprika
- ➢ 8 slices bacon, cut in half crosswise
- ➢ Toothpicks

Instructions:

- Preheat your Traeger Grill to 375°F before painting your canvas with amazing flavors. Let it sit and warm while you fill the jalapeño peppers with cheese mixture.

- If desired, remove the seeds and membranes from the jalapeño by halving each one lengthways and scooping out the middle with the back of a spoon.

- In the bowl used for blending, blend the cream cheese until it soft, adding the shredded cheddar cheese, garlic powder, and smoked paprika. Mix until well combined.

- Carefully pipe or spread the cream cheese mixture into each jalapeño half to make them full and smooth.

- Finally, in preparing and arranging of the jalapeños take the bacon halves and wrap each of the stuffed halves and fix it by applying a toothpick.

- Position the jalapeños on the grates of your Traeger in a layer, still stuffed and wrapped. Shut the lid and grill for about 20-25 minutes or until the bacon becomes very crisp and the peppers become soft.

- After grilling these jalapeño peppers, then the next thing to do is to serve them, but you will first need to let them cool for about five minutes. May this warmup your tummy and bring joy to your kitchen, this is so spicy, savory whoa!

Tips:

- o If you find the standard poppers a little on the fiery side, then it's possible to take the seeds and membranes out of the jalapeños or even use mini sweet peppers instead.

- o If you wish to get overcooked bacon, then it's possible to pre-fry the bacon to just slightly underneath the desired crispiness before wrapping the bacon around the jalapeño peppers.

- o You should accompany these grilled jalapeño peppers with some ranch or blue cheese dip.

3.3 Smoked Queso Dip

Serves: 10

Cooking Time: 1 hour

Temperature: 250°F

Smoked queso dip is a scrumptious dish for consumption through tortilla chips, pretzels, and vegetables, which is rich in creamy flavor and smoky aroma. Preparing it on your Traeger Grill which gives it an irresistible smoky under taste, is a whole other level.

Ingredients:

- ➢ 16 ounces Velveeta cheese, cubed
- ➢ 1 cup shredded cheddar cheese
- ➢ 1 can (10 ounces) diced tomatoes with green chilies, drained
- ➢ 1/2 cup diced onion
- ➢ 1/2 cup diced bell pepper
- ➢ 1/4 cup diced pickled jalapeños
- ➢ 1/2 cup cooked and crumbled breakfast sausage or chorizo (optional)
- ➢ 1 teaspoon chili powder
- ➢ 1/2 teaspoon cumin

- ➢ 1/4 teaspoon garlic powder
- ➢ 1/4 teaspoon onion powder
- ➢ Fresh cilantro, chopped, for garnish

Instructions:

- Let the temperature reach about 250 degrees Fahrenheit on the grill before continuing. Let it warm up a bit while measuring the queso dip ingredients.

- Although this dish is traditionally baked in a cast iron skillet, it can also be prepared in a disposable aluminum pan; to assemble, put cubed Velveeta cheese, shredded cheddar cheese, diced tomatoes with green chilies, onion, bell pepper, pickled jalapenos, and cooked and crumbled breakfast sausage or chorizo if using. Spice up each season with chili powder, cumin, garlic powder, and onion powder.

- You should be able to place it directly on the grates of your Traeger Grill to sear the food. Cover the dish and let it get a little smoky for 45-60 minutes while stirring from time to time to ensure the cheese has melted and the dip is hot and bubbling.

- After the smoked queso dip has been grilled, take it off the grill and serve as desired, garnishing it with chopped fresh cilantro, if wished. Enjoy the queso dip warm with your chips, pretzels or whatever you may wished to use to dip in it.

Tips:

- o Add other spices or ingredients to the queso dip using the cooked ground beef, shredded chicken, or black beans according to your preference.

- o If you want more heat, make sure to include more jalapeños cut into cubes or a teaspoon of hot sauce.

- o The queso dip should be served hot, and this can be achieved by keeping the skillet warm on a trivet or warming tray.

- o Any leftover queso dip should be refrigerated in an airtight container for up to three days; to reheat the dip, place the container in the microwave or place on the grill.

3.4 Grilled Nachos

Serves: 8

Cooking Time: 20 minutes

Temperature: 350°F

Grilled Nachos: Cheesy, tangy, and spicy, nachos are an easy to prepare snack of tortilla chips wonderfully garnished with cheese, salsa, and jalapeños. Packed with cheese, beans, meat, and other good stuff for topping, this nacho is roasted well on your Traeger Grill and has that unique smokey taste.

Ingredients:

- ➢ 1 bag (about 10 ounces) tortilla chips
- ➢ 2 cups shredded cheese (such as cheddar or Monterey Jack)
- ➢ 1 can (15 ounces) black beans, drained and rinsed
- ➢ 1 cup diced cooked chicken, beef, or pork (optional)
- ➢ 1/2 cup diced tomatoes
- ➢ 1/4 cup sliced black olives
- ➢ 1/4 cup sliced jalapeños
- ➢ 1/4 cup diced red onion
- ➢ 1/4 cup chopped fresh cilantro
- ➢ Sour cream, guacamole, and salsa for serving

Instructions:

- The first step you want to take is turning on your Traeger Grill to a heat of 350°F. Let it warm up when you are getting ready to prepare your nachos.

- First you should put a thin layer of tortilla chips on a large baking sheet or a disposable aluminum pan. Lightly top half of the chips with the shredded cheese, then layer one half of black beans, chicken (if used), tomatoes, olives, jalapeños, and red onions over this layer. Make more layers of the following: Place the rest of the ingredients starting with the cream.

- Put the assembled nachos directly on the grill grates of your Traeger or place the joes on the grill and then put the nachos on top. Lift the lid and grill further for 15-20 minutes or until the cheese turns soft and sizzling.

- After the grilled nachos has taken the desired color, transfer them into a serving dish and garnish with chopped fresh cilantro. Garnish with a side of sour cream, guacamole, and salsa for one delicious dish.

Tips:

- o Depending on your preference, you can load it up with options like cooked ground beef or chicken chips, diced avocado, or pickled jalapeño.

- o To add extra seasoning taste, you can apply taco seasoning for the nachos before cooking them on the grill.

- o Grill the Nachos to serve in parties as appetizers and snack or as a meal during informal occasions.

3.5 Smoked Deviled Eggs

Serves: 12

Cooking Time: 30 minutes

Temperature: 180°F

Smoked deviled eggs are an extra step beyond the traditional deviled eggs that can be taught to others and served at functions. From the preparation up to the final stage of cooking the eggs on the Traeger Grill gives the creamy filling that almost smoky taste which is incredibly delicious.

Ingredients:

- ➢ 12 large eggs
- ➢ 1/2 cup mayonnaise
- ➢ 2 tablespoons Dijon mustard
- ➢ 1 tablespoon white vinegar
- ➢ 1/4 teaspoon salt
- ➢ 1/4 teaspoon black pepper
- ➢ Smoked paprika, for garnish
- ➢ Chopped fresh chives, for garnish

Instructions:

- • Prepare Traeger Grill for the cooking by setting it to a preheat temperature of

180 degrees F. It should be allowed to heat while the eggs are prepared.

- Before boiling water, crack the eggs and put them on the grill grates of your Traeger without using any dish. Open the lid and smoke the denim for 30 minutes.

- Begin by boiling down the eggs with salt and once finished that, carefully remove the eggs through smoking and continue cooking them in boiling water for ten minutes.

- After the process is complete, turn off the heat and cool the eggs off completely. Boil the eggs, and once cooked, make sure you crack the shells open, and then use a knife to cut each egg into two halves along the lengthwise direction. Scoop out the yolks from the whites using a spoon and pour them into another bowl. Beat the yolks using a fork to ensure they are fine and of a smooth consistency to make omelets. Make sure to add the mayonnaise, Dijon mustard, white vinegar, salt, and pepper and make sure that they are well combined.

- Using a spoon or a pipe, fill the prepared egg white halves with the yolk mixture to fill each equally and neatly.

- As for the final touches, you can sprinkle the smoked deviled eggs with the smoked paprika and finely chopped fresh chives. Serve chilled and enjoy!

Tips:

o For extra flavor, you can add ingredients such as chopped bacon, diced pickles, or hot sauce to the yolk mixture.

o One should cool the eggs before filling so that the filling does not end up as soft as it fills the egg case.

o Here are the steps to make smoked deviled eggs, including instructions on how to enjoy it as a party food or as a side dish for a hearty brunch or lunch meal. Precisely, people will be fascinated about these kinds of props!

3.6 Grilled Stuffed Mushrooms

Serves: 6

Cooking Time: 25 minutes

Temperature: 375°F

Stuffed mushrooms are quite easy to prepare, and they always go well during parties, especially when served grilled. With your Traeger Grill, these mushrooms are stuffed with cheese, herbs, and breadcrumbs then are grilled to come out perfect.

Ingredients:

- ➤ 24 large button mushrooms
- ➤ 1/4 cup olive oil
- ➤ 2 cloves garlic, minced
- ➤ 1/2 cup breadcrumbs
- ➤ 1/4 cup grated Parmesan cheese
- ➤ 2 tablespoons chopped fresh parsley
- ➤ Salt and pepper to taste
- ➤ 1/4 cup shredded mozzarella cheese

Instructions:

- Prepare your Traeger Grill on the preheat setting for food at 375 degrees Fahrenheit. Let it warm up while you get the mushrooms readjust to the temperature.

- Trim off the stems from the mushrooms and carefully cut out the dark mice colored part with the help of a spoon. In preparing the five items, arrange the mushroom caps on a baking pan covered with aluminum foil.

- In a small frying pan, sauté the olive oil with gentle heat intensity. Put the minced garlic and sauté for 1-2 minutes until the garlic releases aroma. Take off the heat and mix in the breadcrumbs, grated Pariser Cheese, the chopped parsley, salt, and pepper.

- Divide the breadcrumb mixture and spread it atop the mushroom shells, making sure to press them gently to fill the space. Top each stuffed mushroom will shred mozzarella cheese and sprinkle them all over.

- Put the stuffed mushrooms right on the grates of your Traeger to get grilled in this method. Shut the lid and grill for an additional 20-25 minutes, or until the mushrooms become tender and the cheese is melted and bubbly.

- Carefully, pull the grilled stuffed mushrooms off the grill and place it on a serving plate. Which will taste best when served hot Enjoy the tasty goodness of these recipes!

Tips:

- o To the filling of your choice, you can add contributes such as cooked sausage, spinach, bell peppers or any other vegetables of your preference.

- o As an additional option, you can choose to grill the stuffed mushrooms and then finish by broiling it for about 2-5 minutes longer to achieve a crispy top.

- o Grilled stuffed mushrooms are a perfect dish for appetizers or under meat dishes at a meat party.

3.7 Smoked Cheddar Cheese Balls.

Serves: 8

Cooking Time: 1 hour

Temperature: 225°F

Cheese balls made using smoked cheddar cheese is one of the most enticing snacks which can be prepared very easily and can be serve best during parties and game day or any occasions. Using sharp cheddar cheese, cream cheese, and seasonings, this cheese balls are smoked to perfection in your Traeger Grill giving it that attractive smoked flavor you will appreciate.

Ingredients:

- ➢ 8 ounces sharp cheddar cheese, shredded
- ➢ 8 ounces cream cheese, softened
- ➢ 1/4 cup mayonnaise
- ➢ 1/4 cup chopped green onions
- ➢ 1/4 cup chopped pecans
- ➢ 1 tablespoon Worcestershire sauce
- ➢ 1 teaspoon garlic powder
- ➢ 1/2 teaspoon smoked paprika
- ➢ Salt and pepper to taste
- ➢ 1/2 cup chopped pecans or chopped fresh parsley for coating (optional)

Instructions:

- Original temperature setting: Set your Traeger Grill at a temperature of 225°F. Let it heat as you prepare your cheese balls, the heat is important for the cheese to melt properly.

- Shred one cup of sharp cheddar cheese and mix it together with the 8 oz package of cream cheese, half mayonnaise, chopped green onions, chopped pecans, Worcestershire sauce, garlic powder, smoked paprika, salt and the black pepper. Mix until well combined.

- With this, take some quantity of cheese mixture in your hand then form them into small round balls that are about one inch round. For additional garnishing you can coat the cheese ball in chopped pecans, or you can also chop fresh parsley and coat the cheese balls with it.

- So, transfer the shaped cheese balls right on the browning grates of the Traeger that you have. Put the lid on and smoke for one hour or until the cheese balls are firm and developed a slightly golden-brown shade.

- Once the smoked cheddar cheese balls are fully done prepare to take them from the grill and let them cool for a few minutes. Serving Suggestions: Place the wings on a platter with toothpicks for easy piercing and munching and get ready to be amazed by a smoky explosion of taste!

Tips:

o You can mix in other fillings like crumbled cooked bacon, diced jalapeños, or even chopped herbs for a slightly different taste to the cheese balls.

o That way the cream cheese should have been softened enough to allow them to mix properly with the other ingredients and the final product should be smooth and creamy.

o If any cheese balls are remaining, they should be stored in an airtight container and placed in the refrigerator until 3 days elapse. It is very important to reheat them in oven or on the grill for serving.

3.8 Onions and Other Toppings on Grilled Flatbread

Serves: 6

Cooking Time: 15 minutes

Temperature: 400°F

I wanted to come up with a simple dish that is versatile and appealing to most people and would be good for serving for barbeques or just a quick bites idea. It is very versatile, and one can put any type of toppings that one favors, hence making it ideal for everyone. Grill the flatbread to a nice crispness on your Traeger Grill as the smoky flavors mesh well with the other ingredients.

Ingredients:

- ➢ 2 store-bought flatbreads or pizza crusts
- ➢ Olive oil, for brushing
- ➢ Salt and pepper to taste
- ➢ Toppings of your choice (such as tomato sauce, cheese, vegetables, meats, herbs, etc.)

Instructions:

- You need to turn on your Traeger Grill and bring it to 400 degrees Fahrenheit. Let it preheat while you assemble the flat bread and the other items that will go on top.

- Spread oven-ready flatbreads or pizza crust on the baking sheet or pizza peel ready to be baked. Using a pastry brush, brush the tops of the mixture with olive oil and sprinkle with required amount of salt and pepper.

- This should be done on the oiled and seasoned flatbreads after adjusting your toppings to cover the flatbreads as per your preferences. This is the reason why many people prefer to add creative toppings, so that they can mix and match different essence and food materials.

- Gently place all the prepared flatbreads directly on the grating rods of your Traeger grill. Place the lid on the grill and cook for about 10-15 minutes and check the crust color and toppings to see whether they are hot enough.

- After grilling the flatbreads, transfer them to a different surface, and let them cool for a few minutes to enable them to be sliced properly. It has been found to be encouraging to serve this along with hot flavors once ready.

Tips:

- Use your preferred cheese toppings and blend through various tastes to fix your dream pizza. The districts interpretations include margherita (tomato sauce, fresh mozzarella, basil), barbecue chicken (barbecue sauce, grilled chicken, red onions, cilantro), veggie (tomato sauce, mushrooms, bell peppers, onions, olives).

- Be sure to add some of the toppings to the flatbreads grilled as it enhances the flavor of the food being prepared. Live foods like vegetables and meats may be grilled to impart a smokey flavor to your food, while the fruits could also be grilled.

- It is recommended to serve the grilled flatbreads as main course or appetizer or even as a side dish for more options of meal.

3.9 Smoked Nuts

Serves: 10

Cooking Time: 45 minutes

Temperature: 225°F

Smoked nuts indicate nuts that are prepared from the smoke of burning woods, which are in high demand especially during parties, for game, among other times when hungry people want to have something savory to munch. Caramelizing the nuts on your Traeger Grill adds smoky taste that will complement your nuts in a great way.

Ingredients:

- 1-pound mixed nuts (such as almonds, cashews, pecans, and walnuts)
- 2 tablespoons melted butter or olive oil
- 1 tablespoon Worcestershire sauce
- 1 teaspoon garlic powder
- 1 teaspoon onion powder
- 1 teaspoon smoked paprika
- 1/2 teaspoon cayenne pepper (optional)
- Salt and pepper to taste

Instructions:

- Set your Traeger Grill to a temperature of 225 degrees F. Let it sit and come up to temperature while you toast the nuts.

- For the mixed nuts seasoning, follow these steps Place the mixed nuts in a large mixing bowl, pour in melted butter or olive oil, Worcestershire sauce, garlic powder, onion powder, smoked paprika, cayenne pepper (if applicable), salt, and pepper. Stir well up to the point that each nut is covered with the seasoning mixture in question.

- It will help if you lay out the seasoned nuts in a single layer on a baking sheet or a disposable aluminum tray. Put the pan immediately on the grates of the Traeger equipment or grill. If using peanuts, the nuts are ready when toasted and have emitted steam after 45 mins of smoking the lid closed with occasional stirring.

- Once the nuts are well smoked, transfer them out of the grill and allow to cool before eating. They can be consumed on their own as a snack, or included for a crunch factor in salads, trail mixes or even charcuterie boards.

Tips:

- o You can even adjust the seasoning mixture to your own liking, since making it from scratch allows for that kind of flexibility. You can control this with this amount of cayenne pepper but if one wants it hotter you can always add more, or one can try different types of herbs and spices.

- o For the nuts which are not consumed you should store smokers in an airtight jar at room temperature they will last up to a week and a half. They are perfect back in every aspect as a tasty snack whenever one feels like eating!

3.10 Grilled Zucchini Fries

Serves: 6

Cooking Time: 20 minutes

Temperature: 375°F

Grilled zucchini fries are tasty and healthy compared to fried potatoes and can be enjoyed by all persons, especially kids. These were crispy exterior with a melted tender core; moreover, it was herbal and parmesan cheese dusted. Perfect served as appetizers or side dishes of any kind, these are delicious when grilled on the side of your Traeger Grill. :

Ingredients:

- 3 medium zucchinis
- 1/2 cup breadcrumbs
- 1/4 cup grated Parmesan cheese
- 1 teaspoon Italian seasoning
- 1/2 teaspoon garlic powder
- Salt and pepper to taste
- 2 eggs, beaten
- Cooking spray

Instructions:

- Turn your Traeger Grill on and set it to Smoke with the lid closed for about 5 minutes before trying to regulate the temperature, then bring it to 375°F. Let it sit for a while to warm while preparing the zucchini fries.

- Peel off the outer skin of zucchini and chop of its ends then cut it into thin strips like French fries.

- In a separate bowl, prepare the crisp layer, breadcrumbs, grated Parmesan cheese, Italian seasoning, garlic powder, salt, and pepper.

- To prepare the zucchini fry, you need to dip it first into the beaten eggs ensuring that it will be evenly coated. After that, you need to dip it in the breadcrumb mixture and press gently so that it will stick well.

- Place the coated zucchini fries in a neat layer on a baking sheet lined with parchment paper or aluminum foil in a way that they will not be touching each other. The fries could be sprinkled lightly with some cooking spray to facilitate browning.

- Put the baking sheet right on the grill rack of your Traeger for positive outcomes. Lay the fries on the grill and grill for about 10-12 minutes; thereafter, turn on the other side of the fries and grill for further 8-10 minutes until the fries are thoroughly crispy and, golden brown.

- Once you get done with grilling, bring the zucchini fries out and serve hot with marinara sauce, ranch dressing, or aioli.

Tips:

- To achieve the extra crispy zucchini fries, can place a wire rack on the baking-sheet and then lay the fries. This helps to facilitate air to flow on the fries as they cook, thus crisping them up evenly.

- Using your favorite herbs and spices, you are free to adjust the seasoning mixture to suit your preference. Such spices such as smoked paprika, onion powder, or chili powder could add a delicious spice to the fries.

- Enjoy these zucchini fries grilled and consume them as a substitute for regular fries or indulge in them as starters or side dishes to any meals.

Chapter 4: Poultry Perfection

Welcome to the realm of poultry perfection, where chicken, turkey, and more take center stage. Poultry is incredibly versatile, and with your Traeger Grill, you can elevate these everyday proteins into extraordinary meals. This chapter is dedicated to exploring the full potential of grilled and smoked poultry, ensuring every bite is juicy, flavorful, and cooked to perfection.

From the succulent smoked whole chicken that's perfect for family dinners to the tender, flavorful grilled chicken breasts ideal for any occasion, we've got a range of recipes that showcase the best of poultry. You'll also find creative dishes like smoked duck and grilled Cornish hens, bringing gourmet flair to your grill repertoire. Each recipe is designed to highlight the natural flavors of the poultry while adding a smoky depth that only your Traeger can provide. Get ready to master the art of poultry grilling and smoking, turning simple ingredients into show-stopping meals.

4.1 Smoked Whole Chicken

Serves: 6

Cooking Time: 2. 5 hours

Temperature: 225°F

Grilling a whole chicken on the Traeger grill creates a great depth of smoky, tender chicken that can be used in many dishes. And with that, you are going to learn how to cook one of the most delicious meals with not many ingredients and only few minutes on a grill.

Ingredients:

> - 1 whole chicken (about 4-5 pounds)
> - Olive oil
> - Salt and pepper
> - Your favorite poultry seasoning or rub

Instructions:

- First and foremost, you have to get your Traeger Grill ready for cooking by setting its temperature to 225 degrees F. Here, you can use your favorite hardwood pellets for smoking, and they may include hickory, apple, or cherry.

- The first step is to take the chicken out of its packaging and discard the liquid that may have accumulated at the bottom. In the case of the chicken, you just have to drizzle some olive oil and then massage the chicken over the body part of the chicken with the olive oil. Rinse the chicken thoroughly and pat dry; rub both with a generous amount of salt, pepper, and your preferred poultry seasoning/rub for the exterior, and some oil for basting for the inside.

- Put the seasoned whole chicken right on the grill grates of your Traeger, also, with the breast facing up. The lid can now be shut along with smoking for about 2. To 3 hours depending on the size of the chicken, or until the chicken reaches an internal temperature of 165°F in the thickest part of the breast and/or thighs.

- This being the case, after taking the chicken to the required heat, it has to be taken off the grill and place on a chopping board. It is recommended that chicken be allowed to stand and to rest for about 10-15minutes after which it can be carved.

- After that, you can divide the smoked whole chicken into separate pieces and eat it while still hot. Here is a great opportunity to taste the smoky aroma and succulent, juicy meat!

Tips:

- For extra taste, you can season the inside of the chicken with spices and lay ingredients like lemon, garlic, onions, or herbs inside the cavity before smoking.

- To achieve crispy skin, the Traeger Grill temperature can be raised to 375°F after 15-20 minutes of cooking.

- Therefore, remaining smoked chicken can be kept in an air-tight container in a refrigerator for a maximum of three days. It is best taken cold in sandwiches, salads, or rolls, although you can reheat the filled pastries gently under a grill or in a microwave oven.

4.2 Grilled Chicken Breasts

Serves: 4

Cooking Time: 30 minutes

Temperature: 350°F

Chicken on the grill is quite versatile and is always delicious when prepared with barbeque seasoning. In fact, preparing them on your Traeger Grill is one of the ways of preparing them that gives them the best flavor. Here's how to grill chicken breasts to perfection.

Ingredients:

- ➤ 4 boneless, skinless chicken breasts
- ➤ Olive oil
- ➤ Salt and pepper
- ➤ Your favorite seasoning blend or marinade

Instructions:

- This dish recommends preheating the Traeger Grill to a temperature of 350 degrees Fahrenheit. Choose the best hardwood pellets for grilling, considering some of the most popular ones like mesquite, pecan, or oak pellets.

- Take the chicken breasts and put them on a chopping board and rub them with the olive oil. Coat each side of the chicken breasts with salt, pepper, and some other seasonings of your choice or marinate.

- Place the seasoned chicken breasts directly onto the grill grates of your Traeger. Next, you should close the lid and grill for about 6-8 minutes per side, or until fully cooked through with at least 165°F internal temperature and clear juices.

- This is done when the inside of the chicken breasts is adequately cooked when you remove it from the grill and place on a serving platter. After removing the chicken from the oven, it should be allowed to stand for some time before it is cut so that the juices that are trapped inside can redistribute.

- Enjoy the grilled chicken breasts as a meal, which is best served hot with a side dish of your preferred choice including vegetables, rice, or salad. Indulge in the fantastic smoky essences and juicy, succulent meat!

Tips:

- ○ They should never be over cooked to avoid them becoming too hard and not being appealing to the taste buds. Although they shouldn't withstand the tenderness test, it is advisable to use a meat thermometer to confirm that they have reached a core temperature of 165°F.

- o When preparing the grilled chicken, the seasoning may vary depending on the preferences of the chicken lovers as well as the type of seasoning blend or marinades used. Get creative with this recipe and try out your preferred herbs, spices, and sauces to help create delectable meals.

- o Cooked chicken breasts can be kept in the refrigerator for up to 3 days provided the container holding the chicken has been properly sealed. However, they are recommended to be consumed cold; they may be incorporated in sandwiches, salads or wraps but may also be warmed lightly in the oven or a microwave before consumption.

4.3 Turkey Breast Roast

Serves: 8

Cooking Time: 3 hours

Temperature: 225°F

Cooking a turkey breast on a Traeger Grill is an easy way to prepare this type of food, which makes this method ideal for preparing for Thanksgiving at any time of the year. This recipe is perfect for holidays and for other weeks in a week the turkey turns out juicy and has more of a smoky flavor.

Ingredients:

- ➢ 1 whole bone-in turkey breast (about 6-8 pounds)
- ➢ Olive oil
- ➢ Salt and pepper
- ➢ Your favorite poultry seasoning or rub
- ➢ Turkey brine (optional)

Instructions:

- First, set your Traeger Grill on the lowest temperature setting, the one that is approximately 225°F. Preferably, smoke your sweet potato using your favorite hardwood pellets like apple, cherry, or pecan.

- If using, brine the turkey breast according to the instruction provided on the packaging side of the turkey. Take the turkey breast out of the brine and drain it, removing all the excess liquid with paper towels. For instance, place a turkey breast on a plate and pour olive oil over it so that it can evenly cover the entire breast. First, kindly sprinkle the turkey breast with salt, black pepper, and poultry seasoning or any rub of your choice, internal and external.

- Expertly position the seasoned turkey breast right on the grates of the grill on your Traeger with the skin side up. Cover and fume for about 3 to 3. Alternatively, you can boil it for 5 hours or cook it until the inner heat is 165°F on the thickest portion of the breast.

- When the turkey breast is ready, that is when the internal temperature reads the required level, it has to be pulled from the grill and placed on the chopping board. This allows the juices that have fluidized during roasting to redistribute within the turkey breast.

- After smoking the turkey breast, it is cut into slices and served immediately. Have the unique smoky taste and tender juicy meat to your heart's content.

Tips:

- Additionally, for a more enhanced taste, you should consider seasoning inside of the turkey breast by placing lemon, garlic, onions, or fresh herbs before smoking it.

- However, if you wish to have a crispier skin, you can enhance the temperature of the Traeger Grill to about 375 degrees Fahrenheit in the last 15 to 20 minutes of cooking.

- For leftover smoked turkey breast, you can place it in an airtight container and be put in the fridge for 3 days maximum. It is best when served cold, it can be used in sandwiches, salads, and wraps this is perfect for photocopy parties or the office. If you want to reheat, you can do so in an oven or microwave before serving.

4.4 Smoked Duck

Serves: 6

Cooking Time: 4 hours

Temperature: 225°F

Incidentally, smoking a duck on the Traeger Grill turns out tender, juicy, and perfectly crisp on the outside, and I highly recommend this method of preparing duck for festive events or a family dinner. This dish will satisfy any occasion from special to impressing your dinner party guests from Monday to Friday.

Ingredients:

- ➢ 1 whole duck (about 5-6 pounds)
- ➢ Salt and pepper
- ➢ Your favorite poultry seasoning or rub
- ➢ Orange slices, garlic cloves, and fresh herbs for stuffing (optional)

Instructions:

- Before preparing the ribs on the Traeger Grill, you need to set it to 225°F first. Smoking uses your preferred hardwood pellet which include cherry, hickory, or oak.

- Pull out all the things that you find in the cavity of the chicken, the shriveled-up thing and the gizzards and throw them away. After this, pat the duck dry using paper towels, and remove any fatty layer in it by cutting. Draw patterns on the skin of the duck that resembles the crosshatch dressing using a pen or a sharp knife, but do not pierce the flesh of the duck. Truffle oil is great because it permeates throughout and really adds a hint of luxury to the meal, and season the duck heavily with kosher salt, black pepper, and any poultry seasoning or dry rub you prefer on the inside and out. If you would like, season the duck cavity with snippets of oranges, crushed garlic, and the actual fresh herbs.

- Put the seasoned duck on the grill without using any trays or pans: the high side of the Traeger grill should have the breast side up. Close the lid and smoke for about 3 minutes The next step is to – 5 to 4 hours more, or until properly cooked for at least 165 °F inside the thickest part of the breast and thigh.

- When the duck comes to the right temperature on the grill, proceed to take it out carefully and place it on a cutting table. Remove the duck from the oven and allow it to rest for about 15-20 minutes to allow the juices to distribute itself evenly before carving it.

- I will roast the smoked duck and then slice the smoked duck into portions for consumption when hot. Savor the smoky taste and moister flavors of these tender fried meats!

Tips:

- For more taste you can, before the last 30 minutes, baste it with honey ginger, soy, and orange juice.

- Serve the smoked duck with your favorite sides, such as roasted vegetables, wild rice, or a fresh salad, for a complete meal.

- Refrigeration is the best way to save the remaining smoked duck as it can be kept in an airtight container in the fridge for a period not exceeding 72 hours. It is best served cold on salads or sandwiches, or warm with heating in the oven or microwave before consumption.

4.5 Grilled Chicken Thighs

Serves: 4

Cooking Time: 35 minutes

Temperature: 375°F

Cooked chicken thighs on the grill are a one-of-a-kind scrumptious chicken that is suitable for all moments. This is perfect when you're cooking for dinner or even a barbecue, your chicken would be perfectly moist and the smokiness simply fantastic.

Ingredients:

- 8 bone-in, skin-on chicken thighs
- Olive oil
- Salt and pepper
- Your favorite seasoning blend or marinade

Instructions:

- When cooking in your Traeger Grill you should preheat them to about 375 degrees Fahrenheit. But when grilling or barbequing you may opt to use your favorite hardwood pellets like mesquite, apple, or pecan.

- Arrange the pieces of chicken thighs in a cutting board and remove excess moisture from these chicken pieces with the help of paper towels. In a bowl, wet the chicken thighs with olive oil and assure that each piece is covered. Maine guidelines to season the chicken thighs are to sprinkle salt, pepper, and any preferred seasoning mix or marinade on both the exterior and the inside of the skin.

- Shove the seasoned chicken thighs, up to the grates of your Traeger, with the skin side facing down. Pour the lid and grill for about 15-20min before flipping the thighs and then grill them for 15-20min more or until they're tender, their juices can be cleared and the temperature touch 165°F.

- This is done once the chicken thighs are well cooked; they are, therefore, taken off the grill and served on a platter. After that, let the chicken thighs stay for a few minutes and then serve, this is because the juices need to be redistributed.

- Enjoy the Grilled Chicken Thighs hot as an accompaniment to the side dishes which may be Receptors such as vegetables, cooked rice, or salad. Indulge in the smokiness and moist, succulent touch!

Tips:

- To add some extra taste, marinate the chicken thighs in desired marinade of your choice and leave it aside for about 4 hours before grilling.

- For more crispy skin, you can raise the temperature of the Traeger Grill to 400F degrees during the last 5-10 minutes of grilling.

- Eaten chicken thighs can be stored in a fridge in an airtight container for 3 days at most. Consume them chilled with sandwiches, salads or wraps or to warm them slightly in an oven or Microwave for like a sandwich.

4.6 Smoked Turkey Legs

Serves: 4

Cooking Time: 3 hours

Temperature: 250°F

Do you know that turkey legs roasted at the fair surroundings is something you can easily prepare at home using Traeger Grill? I doubt you will not use these delicious smoked turkey legs for your barbecuing events or other celebration.

Ingredients:

> ➤ 4 turkey legs
> ➤ Olive oil
> ➤ Salt and pepper
> ➤ Your favorite poultry seasoning or rub

Instructions:

- Prepare your Traeger Grill for low temperature grilling by setting the temperature control dials to 250 degrees Fahrenheit. So here we decide on the type and brand of hardwood pellets preferred for smoking which include hickory, cherry, and oak.

- Rinse the turkey legs with cold water, and blot today with the help of paper towels; it is also useful to cut off the unnecessary pieces of skin and fat. Season the turkey legs with olive oil and ensure that it covers the legs so that the//@prescribe oil can spread evenly when grilling. With a small sharp knife, trim any excess fat off the legs and dry the skin with paper towels, then season with salt, pepper and your preferred poultry seasoning, or RUB endorsed.

- Sit the seasoned turkey legs right on the grates of your Traeger with no use of the basket or roasting pan. Turn off the heat and cover the lid for about 2. 5 to 3 hours, until the internal temperature in its thickest part reaches 165°F as is the case of the legs.

- The turkey legs should be thoroughly cooked on the grill; subsequently, you should remove them and place them on a serving platter. Take some time out to allow the turkey legs to cool down slightly, this will ensure the juices can be evenly distributed.

- Enjoy your smoked turkey legs steaming hot with your preferred side items of cooked mash potatoes, corn bread or a tossed salad and coleslaw. By killing the birds, people also get to eat tasty smoky tasty and juicy poultry.

Tips:

- As an enhancement of flavor, it is advisable to use a liquid solution of water, salt, and sugar with additional compounds that you can inject into the turkey legs for a period of 8 to 12 hours before smoking.

- If you want a crispy skin, then you can grill them on high heat for a few minutes or put the turkey legs in the oven and broil at 375°F for about 10-15 minutes.

- When you are left with a smoked turkey leg, they can be wrapped and packed in an airtight container, ensuring that it lasts for up to three days in the refrigerator. You can consume them as cold dishes – in salads, sandwiches, etc., or warm them up in the oven or in the microwave, but don't fry them.

4.7 Grilled Cornish Hens

Serves: 4

Cooking Time: 1 hour

Temperature: 350°F

I have found that the following recipe of grilled Cornish hens is spicy and tasty that can be served during parties, meetings, family gatherings, or even on holidays. Whether you're having a small celebration or just craving some delicious and juicy poultry, these small birds do not take long to cook on your Traeger Grill.

Ingredients:

- 4 Cornish hens
- Olive oil
- Salt and pepper
- Your favorite poultry seasoning or rub
- Fresh herbs for garnish (optional)

Instructions:

- Before we start cooking, turn your Traeger Grill on and set it to 350 degrees Fahrenheit. For grilling, we recommend the hardwood of your choice – apple, pecan, or maple.

- It is also important to wash with cold water and dry it using the paper towel before proceeding to the next step. Lightly coat the hens with olive oil using a brush spread the oil on the hens' skin. Rinse the hens and pat them dry before heavily seasoning them with your preferred combination of salt, black pepper, and poultry seasoning or any desired poultry rub, inside and out. I have indicated that it is advisable to stuff the cavity of each hen with fresh herbs such as thyme, rosemary, or sage to enrich the flavor of the chicken.

- Grab the seasoned Cornish hens and place them right on the grate of the grill without a plate, with the breast side up. This can be achieved by closing the lid and grilling it for about 45 minutes to one hour or until the meat on the breast and thigh read an internal temperature of 165°F.

- When the Cornish hens are ready to be grilled and they are fully cooked, then, gently, you are supposed to pull them off the grill and then place them on the serving plate. One of the ways of serving the hens is allowing them to rest for several minutes thus allowing the juices to spread again.

- Baste the grilled Cornish hens hot when served with side orders of vegetables, potatoes, or wild rice of your preference. It can be served with additional fresh herbs if preferred and highly recommended to enjoy the taste of the preparations.

Tips:

o This is especially good if you would like to have a crispy skin while cooking this in the Traeger Grill, you can raise its heat to 400 degrees F to the last 10-15minutes of cooking.

o Refrigerated grilled Cornish hens may be eaten after they have been stored in an airtight container for up to three days. It is ideal for using them cold, to accompany salads, sandwiches, or rolls; however, it can also be defrosted gently in the oven or microwave and served warm.

4.8 Smoked Chicken Drumsticks

Serves: 6

Cooking Time: 1. 5 hours

Temperature: 225°F

Barbecued chicken is a colorful, flavorful, and delicious item that is best suited for any type of event such as barbecues, football matches or any type of event that may come along. Grill it low and slow on your Traeger grill for that smoky flavor by soaking it into the meat making it juicy and tender.

Ingredients:

- ➢ 12 chicken drumsticks
- ➢ Olive oil
- ➢ Salt and pepper
- ➢ Your favorite poultry seasoning or rub
- ➢ Barbecue sauce (optional, for serving)

Instructions:

- Set the temperature of your Traeger Grill to about 225 F. Ideally, try using your preferred hardwood pellets for smoking and include hickory, mesquite, or cherry types.

- To continue, first, remove the chicken drumsticks from the packaging then wash them with cold water and dried with a paper towel. First, rinse the drumsticks and pat them dry with a paper towel; Then, pour olive oil over the drumsticks and massage it evenly on the skin of the chicken. Using the same seasoning that the drumsticks were first seasoned with, sprinkle it over the drumsticks and rub it in well and make sure they are seasoned well on all sides.

- Arrange the seasoned chicken drumsticks directly on the grates of the grill of your Traeger without using the rack or pan. Close the lid and smoke for around 1: With the lid closed, you would smoke your food for around one hour. 5 to 2 hours, or just until the internal temperature of the drumsticks registers at 165 degrees F.

- To prepare chicken drumstick skewers, it's essential to ensure that the chicken is adequately grilled, so once the chicken drumsticks are cooked, one should carefully decide to remove them from the grill and arrange them on a serving plate. You can also brush it with barbecue sauce for extra flavor if you fancy. There is nothing like bao but to eat it hot and have that smoky experience!

Tips:

- ○ Before smoking, the chicken drumsticks can be seasoned with barbeque sauce or preferred marinade for an extra flavor possible up to four hours.

- o If you want to have tender skin, you can broil the drumsticks for the last 5-10 minutes right on the grill or put in pre-heated oven at 375°F for the last 5-10 minutes.

- o The preparation of smoked chicken drumsticks can be made ahead of time leftover can be stored in an airtight container in the refrigerator and can be consumed up to 3 days. You may eat the meat cold in salads, sandwiches or wrapped, or warm them in the oven or using microwave to warm them up gently.

4.9 Grilled Chicken wings with barbeque sauce

Serves: 6

Cooking Time: 45 minutes

Temperature: 375°F

This grilled chicken wings with BBQ sauce is one of the most popular wings you can offer to your family friends and relatives during party or during weekends, game days, and even weekdays. This means that if you opt for preparing them in your Traeger Grill, you will be able to have Smoky taste and texture that is Tender and Juicy.

Ingredients:

- ➤ 3 lbs chicken wings, split at joints, tips removed
- ➤ Olive oil
- ➤ Salt and pepper
- ➤ Your favorite BBQ sauce
- ➤ Optional: additional seasonings or rubs for extra flavor

Instructions:

- Plug in your Traeger Grill, fire it up, and set it to the smoke stage at 375°F. Choose your preferred hardwood pellets to use when grilling like hickory, apple, or mesquite etc.

- To prepare chicken wings you need to pat them dry with the help of any kind of paper and put them in big bowl. Finally, pour olive oil over it, and sprinkle a lot of salt and black pepper, you can add any spices and herbs, or just your favorite barbecue seasoning or a rub.

- Place the seasoned chicken wings on the grill grates of the Traeger in a single layer and make sure they are not piled on one another. If you're using a charcoal grill, place the wings on the outer rim of the grill and shut the lid, cooking them for about 30-35 minutes while flipping halfway through until the meat is no longer pink and wings are crisp on the outside.

- Before removing the chicken wings from the grill, paint the wings with your preferred barbecue sauce and ensure all the wings are well covered. Place the lid on the grill and close the lid and cook for about another 5-10 minutes or until the sauce is thick and becomes sticky.

- Turn over the chicken wings and grill the other side for some more time Take out the chicken wings from the grill and place on a serving dish. Enjoy it warm with additional BBQ sauce on the side to drizzle over your slice, and side dishes of your choice such as coleslaw, corn bread or potato salad. Crank it up and get that sizzling, smoky flavor and that good old' finger-licking experience!

Tips:

- To get extra crispy wings, it is advisable to use the Traeger Grill and set it at 400°F in the final 5-10 minutes of the grilling time.

- You can also add more detailed additional ingredients like honey, garlic, hot sauce, additional spice etc. to your BBQ sauce depending on your taste bud.

- The procedure to follow as concerns storage of the leftover grilled chicken wings is as follows; the wings can be stored in an airtight container in the refrigerator where it can last for up to 3 days. You can also heat them again in the oven or grill just before serving to retain the crunchiness offered by the toppings.

4.10 Smoked Chicken Tenders

Serves: 4

Cooking Time: 30 minutes

Temperature: 350°F

Smoked chicken tenders with recipe are tremendously tender and outstanding dish that can be prepared for lunch, dinner or as an appetizer for a party. Cook them on your Traeger Grill and you can add smoky flavors to them while remaining soft inside.

Ingredients:

- ➤ 1 lb chicken tenders
- ➤ Olive oil
- ➤ Salt and pepper
- ➤ Your favorite seasoning blend or rub

Instructions:

- For preheating Traeger Grill, set it to 350°F. Fire up the smoker with your preferred hardwood pellets for smoking like oak, maple, or cherry.

- I put the chicken tenders under paper towels and place them in a bowl to drain and make it somehow drier. Lightly drizzle with olive oil and provide salting and peppering appropriately as well as using a preferred spice mixture or marinade for tenderizing all the tender meat pieces.

- Place the Chicken tenders seasoned on the grates of the Traeger Grill in one layer. For about 25 to 30 minutes, or until they turn golden brown, and the chicken is no longer pink in the center and reaches 165°F internal temperature, keep the lid closed and smoke.

- Once it is done remove the chicken tenders from the smoker and place it in desired serving dish or plate. Enjoy your ribs smoking hot with barbeque sauce, honey mustard, ranch seasonings, with accompaniments of coleslaw, potato salad or grill vegetables of your choice. Open fire cooking gives that smoky flavor that is irresistible and of course juicy and tender meat.

Tips:

- ○ If desired, use any preferred marinade to apply to the chicken tenders and allow them to set for 1-2 hours before smoking the food item.

- ○ You can use any seasonings of your choice, or you can update the seasoning or the rub to your personal preferences. You can also use different herbs, spices, and seasonings to improve and develop new and better tastes.

- In case you have smoked chicken tenders remaining, they can be resealed in an airtight pack and kept in the refrigerator to be used within the next three days. You can eat them cold for example in salads, roll it in a wrap or sandwich, or cook it again in a low heat using the oven or microwave before eating.

Chapter 5: Beef Bonanza

Get ready to dive into a beef bonanza, where hearty, robust flavors reign supreme. Beef lovers, this chapter is for you. We're talking about juicy ribeye steaks, tender smoked brisket, and everything in between. With your Traeger Grill, you can bring out the rich, savory flavors of beef like never before.

Whether you're preparing a classic smoked brisket for a special occasion or grilling up some beef kebabs for a weekend barbecue, we've got the recipes that will make your grill the star of the show. Explore the deep, complex flavors of smoked meatloaf, enjoy the mouthwatering taste of grilled T-bone steaks, and savor the perfect combination of spices and smoke in our beef ribs.

This chapter is all about celebrating beef in all its glory. Each recipe is designed to maximize flavor and tenderness, ensuring every bite is a delicious experience. So, let's fire up the grill and embark on a beef-filled journey that promises satisfaction in every dish.

5.1 Classic Smoked Brisket

Serves: 10

Cooking Time: 10-12 hours

Temperature: 225°F

It should also be mentioned that smoked briskets are popular within the barbecue culture, as they possess a dense, succulent texture and an intense, smoky flavor. Although it can take a while to have the plants produce the leaves and grow the roots, it is all quite satisfying in the end.

Ingredients:

> ➢ 1 whole beef brisket, about 12-14 pounds, trimmed
> ➢ Your favorite beef rub or seasoning
> ➢ Wood chips or pellets, such as oak or hickory
> ➢ Optional: beef broth or apple juice for spritzing

Instructions:

- First and foremost, set it to the desired temperature of 225 degrees on your Traeger Grill. Smoking also requires the use of the preferred hardwood pellets, which include oak, hickory, and mesquite.

- Following this, remove any excess flesh from the brisket, while retaining some thickness of fat layer to about 1/4 of an inch. Rub the cut with your preferred beef seasoning and ensure each surface of the brisket is entirely covered.

- Position the seasoned brisket on the grill grate finish side up on your Traeger.

Shut the lid and smoke for about 10-12 hours, or until the internal temperature is 195-205ºF and meat is tender using a probe or a fork.

- If wished, you can moisten the brisket every 1-2 hours with beef broth or apple juice for that added taste and to keep the meat juicy.

- When the ultimate is cooked, make sure you take it off the grill and place it on a chopping board. You should also cover the brisket with foil and allow the meat to rest for about 30 minutes to an hour so that the juices circulate evenly throughout the meat.

- The brisket should be sliced crosswise against the grain into thin slices; it must be served hot with barbecue sauce, pickles, onions, and bread/rolls. Indulge in the succulent unctuous of original smoked brisket recipes!

Tips:

- There are few food items that can be prepared in the same way and at the same time, it could take a number of hours before the best results are achieved, and this is why patience is important especially when preparing a smoked brisket. Slow cooking of foods at 225 F is an effective way of producing tender collar bones since it gives ample time to the collagen to dissolve and the meat to develop great flavors.

- This will assist in checking the body temperature of the brisket to determine whether it is properly cooked or cooked to the recommended temperature.

- After the smoked brisket has cooled down to room temperature, you can wrap it tightly in aluminum foil and store in a refrigerator for 3 to 4 days. Ideally, it should be eaten cold and is well suited for sandwiches, salads, or wraps, however it also tastes great if served warm, just heat gently in the oven or microwave.

5.2 Grilled Ribeye Steaks

Serves: 4

Cooking Time: 15 minutes

Temperature: 450°F

Everyone loves their rib eye steaks well-grilled especially if they ordered in a restaurant and in this tutorial, you would learn how to prepare this delicious meal using your Traeger grill. It is when they are grilled to crusty outside and soft and juicy inside especially if done on hot or high grilling.

Ingredients:

➢ 4 boneless ribeye steaks, about 1 inch thick
➢ Olive oil
➢ Salt and pepper
➢ Your favorite steak seasoning or rub

Instructions:

● Position your Traeger Grill to 450°F if it hasn't been used in a while so that it can heat evenly. It is used for grilling, and you should ensure that you are using the right grade hardwood pellets such as oak, hickory or mesquite.

● First, you should prepare the ribeye steaks: pat them dry with paper towels and lightly brush their surfaces with olive oil. Well, first time you marinate your steaks by seasoning it properly with salt, pepper, and your preferred steak seasoning or steak rub salt seasoning on each side.

● When prepared, position the seasoned ribeye steaks directly on the grill grates of your Traeger. Shut the lid and grill for 6-7 minutes on each side and for the steaks that are perfectly grilled, there is a guideline to follow. When preparing a steak to be medium-rare you should try and achieve 130-135°F and if preparing medium steak, you should try and get 135-145°F.

● After ensuring the steaks are well done, use a pair of tongs to move the steaks to another flat surface such as a cutting board. After cooking, let the steaks sit for a few minutes to relax so that the juices can set back in the steaks.

● Bring the ribeye steaks to room temperature before grilling it, and then slice the steaks thinly across the grain before serving; accompany it with your preferred side dishes including roasted vegetables, mashed potatoes, or a fresh salad. This post is packed with readers' favorite recipes for delighting yourself with the tasty and juicy grilled ribeye steaks!

Tips:

○ Ideally, the ribeye steaks you'll be grilling should be brought to room temperature before grilling.

- o Allowing the steaks to rest after grilling is an ideal step since it enhances the even distribution of juices within a steak, thus making it tastier as well as softer.

- o Whichever method you use, those perfectly grilled ribeye steaks can be kept in an airtight container in the refrigerator for up to 3-4 days. It is best to eat them cold incorporating in sandwiches, salads or wraps & can also be reheated gently in the oven/Microwave before consumption.

5.3 Smoked Meatloaf

Serves: 6

Cooking Time: 2 hours

Temperature: 250°F

This recipe for smoked meatloaf will make one delicious dish which would be great for serving to a family or a group of friends during a meal. Due to the special treatment, it receives when cooked on this grill, the meat is moist and tender with a distinct smoky flavor.

Ingredients:

- ➢ 2 lbs ground beef (80/20 blend)
- ➢ 1 cup breadcrumbs
- ➢ 1/2 cup milk
- ➢ 2 eggs, beaten
- ➢ 1/2 cup diced onion
- ➢ 1/2 cup diced bell pepper
- ➢ 2 cloves garlic, minced
- ➢ 1/4 cup ketchup
- ➢ 2 tablespoons Worcestershire sauce
- ➢ 1 tablespoon Dijon mustard
- ➢ Salt and pepper to taste
- ➢ Your favorite barbecue sauce (optional, for glazing)

Instructions:

- • Preheat Traeger Grill: Turn your Traeger grill on and set the temperature to

250 degrees Fahrenheit. When smoking, make sure you are using your preferred hardwood pellets for the process such as oak, hickory and apple pellet.

- Put the ground beef with the breadcrumbs, milk, beaten eggs, diced onion, bell pepper, minced garlic, ketchup, Worcestershire sauce, Dijon mustard, salt, and black pepper into a large bowl and mix them well. Proceed with mixing until all the ingredients have been well incorporated, and the consistency is evenly distributed.

- Place the meatloaf mixture on a baking sheet or spoon it into a greased parchment paper-lined loaf pan. Here, you should compact and shape the mixture into a loaf-shape, ensuring that the shape and size are evenly formed.

- A beef meatloaf can be placed at the grill grates of your Traeger with no interference of any sorts. After that, close the lid and smoke for 10-15 minutes depending on what is desired. 5 to 2 hours to get tender as the meat thermometer inserted in the thickest part of the meat provides 160 °F.

- Alternatively, you can also apply your preferred barbecue sauce during the last ten to fifteen minutes of cooking so that the sauce caramelizes on the smoked meatloaf's surface, giving it a glossy sheen and additional flavor.

- But if you completed cooking the meatloaf, the next step is to take it off the grill and let it set for 10-15 minutes before serving. It helps in redistributing the juices and to be sure that there is a tender meatloaf on the table.

- It is recommended that the smoked meatloaf should be cut into thick piece which should be served hot, accompanied with mashed potatoes, roasted vegetables, or green beans. Please sit back and enjoy this tasty smoked meatloaf which is quite healthy to boot.

Tips:

- One of the ways in which you can make changes to the meatloaf mixture is by including ingredients like chopped bacon, shredded cheese, diced jalapenos among others.

- The remaining smoked meatloaf must be refrigerated and placed in a sealed container so that it can only be consumed in 3-4 days. Sauté it and serve it cold in sandwiches or rolls, or reheat the slices gently in a low oven, or in the microwave.

5.4 Smoked Beef Ribs

Serves: 6

Cooking Time: 6 hours

Temperature: 225°F

Among barbecued food items, smoked beef ribs are one mouthwatering delicacy that is special and mouthwatering with a tasty and juicy taste. This preparation in the Traeger Grill see the meat are slow cooked and tenderized on its surface to create a juicy and flavorful piece of meat.

Ingredients:

- 3 racks beef back ribs
- Your favorite beef rub or seasoning
- Wood chips or pellets, such as oak, hickory, or mesquite

Instructions:

- Prepare your Traeger Grill to the desired temperature with the instructed temperature being 225°F. However, when smoking the ribs, you only need that rich, hardwood smoke flavor, and therefore use oak, hickory, or mesquite pellets.

- It helps to scrape the cooking surface using a knife to loosen the membrane on the back of the beef ribs, then tearing the membrane off. Remove any unnecessary fat if preferred Most frozen beef can be cooked using the following procedures, depending on the time available. Prepare beef ribs with your desired beef rub or cooking seasoning on all the surfaces of the ribs.

- Arrange the beef ribs seasoned on their bones and firmly place them bone-side down on the grates of your Traeger grill. Slam the lid shut and smoke for 5-6 hours or until tender and the meat is starting to pull away from the bone.

- In preparing this meal, after the beef ribs have been grilled, transfer them away from the grill and let it sit for about 10 – 15 minutes before carving. This creates space to have the juices spread out and makes the texture to be juicy and soft.

- After about 3 hours, remove the smoked beef ribs and cut them into neat portions along the bones to ensure they are more tender and easier to eat, the barbecue sauce can be served separately on the side. Tender, explosive with the fragrance of spices and juices, smoked beef ribs are a true delight that can fill your table!

Tips:

- A few kicks of frail & bold ecstasy – glaze over the beef ribs in the mid of the cooking process add a few splashes of beef broth or apple juice before closing the aluminum foil and putting it back to the grill.

- Smoked beef ribs that you didn't consume immediately should be wrapped up well and placed in an airtight container where it should be put in the refrigerator where it should last for 3-4 days. These can be eaten cold toppings on bread, or used in sandwiches, or may be warmed slightly in the oven or microwave.

5.5 Smoked Pork Shoulder

Serves: 8

Cooking Time: 10-12 hours

Temperature: 225°F

Well, smoked pork shoulder also called is a pork butt is one of the key items for a barbecue party. When cooked on your Traeger grilling for a long time at low heat, the meat is tender and juicy, with a smoky taste.

Ingredients:

- 1 bone-in pork shoulder, about 8-10 pounds
- Your favorite pork rub or seasoning
- Wood chips or pellets, such as apple, cherry, or hickory

Instructions:

- Prepare your Digital Control Pro Grill for Traeger by setting the temperature to 225 degrees Fahrenheit. When smoking, you prefer using your preferred hardwood pellet type such as apple, cherry, or hickory.

- Pork shoulder should be trimmed well but leave a layer of fat that will act as the insulating layer helping the fat meat cook properly. A word of advice: coat the pork shoulder very well with whatever type of rub you are using, or any type of seasoning you prefer, on all sides of the meat.

- Position the seasoned pork shoulder right on the grate of your Traeger, sear side up, or the thickest part of the pork shoulder is touching the heat. Shut the cover and smoke with a minimum of 10-12 hours, or until the temperature is in the range of 195-205°F and the meat can easily pull apart.

- When the pork shoulder is cooked to perfection, it is best to plate it by transferring it to a chopping board or any platter you have on hand. Afterwards for the juices to sort out, it is left to rest for between 30 minutes and 1 hour. Pulled pork can also be shredded using two forks or meat claws to ensure the pork shoulder is in bite sizes.

- Served the smoked pork shoulder hot with additional barbecue sauce from the one listed below on the side. You can also get creative and eat it between two slices of bread, folded in a tortilla, or layered on top of nachos or other chips, or simply with barbeque meats or on the side with barbeque accessories such as coleslaw, baked beans, cornbread, etc.

Tips:

- Additionally, for even more enhanced taste, one can marinate the pork shoulder with apple juice, cider vinegar, and different seasonings and inject the shoulder with this mix before the seasoning and smoking processes.

- When there is some leftover smoked pork shoulder, they should be wrapped well and kept in an airtight container in the chillier for about 3-4 days mostly. It is perfect when heated in the microwave or in oven or when used as ingredients in preparing other meals that entail using leftovers, such as the pulled pork sandwiches or tacos.

5.6 Grilled Lamb Chops

Serves: 4

Cooking Time: 15 minutes

Temperature: 400°F

Grilled lamb chops marinated in olive oil, thyme, garlic, and rosemary are great for a special dinner or when you are feeding guests. They go well marinating then grilled on your Traeger because the smokey flavor enhances the natural taste of the lamb.

Ingredients:

> - 8 lamb loin chops, about 1 inch thick
> - Olive oil
> - Salt and pepper
> - Your favorite herb seasoning or rub (optional)

Instructions:

- The Traeger Grill is set to a temperature of 400 degrees Fahrenheit or the medium-high heat setting. You should preferably use hardwood pellets for grilling purposes for instance the oak, hickory, and cherry pellets.

- Remove as much fat as possible from the chops while still leaving a thin layer of fat on the surface, then pat the loin chops dry with paper and brush lightly with olive oil. Rinse the lamb chops and pat them dry before seasoning with black pepper, the specified amount of salt, and your preferred herb marinade/rub, to coat the chops on all surfaces.

- Arrange the lamb chops seasoned in the grill grates of your Traeger without arranging them on any type of plate well. Shut the lid and cook for 3-4 mins each side for medium rare or until the internal temperature is about 130-135 degrees Fahrenheit; about 5-6 mins each side for medium until reach an internal temperature of 140-145 degrees Fahrenheit.

- When the lamb chops are well fried, ensure that you transfer them on to a cooler part of the grill and let them stand for some time before being served out. Thus, the juice spreads and achieves the succulent leisure that makes it tender.

- Enjoy this grilled lamb chops while hot, and they are best served with any of the following side dishes, roasted vegetables, couscous, fresh green salad. It's good to have succulent, tender flavored grilled lamb chops with sometimes.

Tips:

- Lamb chops are best cooked to a medium-rare and therefore should not be cooked for long.

- Lamb chops require short time in the kitchen once cooked it is advisable to present it immediately.

- To make the chops more tender and juicier, you may want to season and marinate the chops with olive oil, garlic, lemon juice, and herbs several hours before grilling.

- Cold grilled lamb chops are good to be stored and eaten for the next 3-4 days in a fridge by putting in an airtight container. It is preferable to serve them cold, for example in salads or sandwiches; however, they may be warmed in a low temperature oven or microwave.

5.7 Grilled Beef Kebabs

Serves: 6

Cooking Time: 15 minutes

Temperature: 400°F

Beef kebabs are incredibly tasty and satisfying meals highly appreciated during barbecues or grill cookouts and normal dinners. Grilling them in your Traeger Grill ensures that even the meat and the vegetables get the smoky flavor you will love; it also turns into a good dish of barbecued meat on a stick.

Ingredients:

- 2 lbs beef sirloin or tenderloin, cut into 1-inch cubes
- 2 bell peppers, any color, cut into chunks
- 1 large red onion, cut into chunks
- 8-10 cherry tomatoes
- Wooden or metal skewers
- Olive oil
- Salt and pepper
- Your favorite steak seasoning or marinade (optional)

Instructions:

- Grab your Traeger Grill and turn it on to high heat setting, about 400 degrees Fahrenheit. To grill, it is advisable to recommend your preferable hardwood pellets which include oak, hickory, or mesquite.

- So, arrange beef cubes, bell pepper chunks, onions chunks, and cherry tomatoes on the skewer with beef cubes, peppers, onions, and tomatoes in between. Spacing: It is advisable to leave a small gap between each piece to ensure equal baking or grilling time. Well, before grilling the kebabs, will lightly oil with olive oil and immediately sprinkle with adequate salt, ground black pepper and your favorite steak seasoning or marinade if you used any.

- Arrange the skewered kebabs on the grill of your Traeger, without using any trays or pans. This is followed by sealing the lid and grilling the kebabs for 10-12 minutes while occasionally flipping the kebabs or until the beef reaches your preferred level of doneness and the vegetables blushing reddish brown.

- After grilling the kebabs, using gloves safely turn them over, and place them on a serving tray. Ideally served hot with accompaniments such as rice, couscous, or a crisp salad on the side. Fully embrace the taste and mouth feel of tasty grilled beef kebabs!

Tips:

- This is to make sure that they do not burn when you are barbecuing, therefore, it is advised that wooden skewers be submerged in water for at least 30 minutes to be used for this purpose.

- To further suit one's preference, other vegetables can be added alongside marinated and grilled kebabs comprising of mushrooms, zucchini, or cherry tomatoes.

- Any leftover grilled beef kebabs should be wrapped well using an aluminum foil and placed in an airtight container inside the refrigerator where it can be stored for 3- 4 days maximum. They are perfect served cold in salads, or wrapped in a taco; however, they can also be tastefully reheated in the oven or the microwave.

5.8 Smoked Tri-Tip Roast

Serves: 8

Cooking Time: 2. 5 hours

Temperature: 225°F

This is a classic recipe that you can prepare for a special occasion or any dinner party since the smoked tri-tip roast is not only tasty but also fancy looking dish. In conclusion, slow cooking in a Traeger Grill provides tastier and juicy result and the smokey flavor enhances the meal.

Ingredients:

> - 1 tri-tip roast, about 4-5 pounds
> - Olive oil
> - Your favorite beef rub or seasoning
> - Wood chips or pellets, such as oak, hickory, or mesquite

Instructions:

- There are two types of preparation I suggest for your Traeger Grill; first, Preheat at 225 Degree F. You will want to smoke your meat with a preferred hardwood pellet, some common ones include oak, hickory, or mesquite.

- Clean the tri-tip roast with paper towels and season it with olive oil by lightly rubbing it on the surface. If no seasoning was applied when the roast was cut, then season the roast heavily with your choice of beef rub or beef seasoning before placing it on the stove.

- Set the seasoned tri-tip roast directly on the grill grates of your Traeger without a need to use a rack. cover it and bake for about 2. It takes about 5-3 hours or until it is thoroughly cooked; medium-rare beef has an internal temperature of 130-135 °F, while the medium beef has 140-145 °F as suggested by using a meat thermometer.

- Once the tri-tip roast is cooked to the desired temperature, pull it out of the grill by using a pair of tongs, and place it on a cutting board. Allow it to stand for 10-15 minutes then serve it sliced in thin slices against the direction of the grain.

- It tastes best when served hot; one can accompany it with side orders like boiled or roasted potatoes, grilled vegetables, or a crisp salad. Got to love the softness of the tri-tip roast while it comes with a robust taste coming from the smoke.

Tips:

- o The tri-tip roast is a piece of beef that isn't too fatty, thus it's important not to overcook the cut so that it doesn't turn into something very chewy and dry.

- The remaining smoked tri-tip roast should be wrapped and placed in a container or plastic wrap and stored in the refrigerator up to 3-4 days. This speed alongside being served warm, also works very well when served cold in sandwiches or salads.

5.9 Grilled T-Bone Steaks

Serves: 4

Cooking Time: 15 minutes

Temperature: 450°F

This amazing recipe complements the delicious T-bone steaks that many diners who love to dine at steakhouse restaurants would enjoy at their homes using the Traeger Grill. Grilling it also grills it over high heat which forms a beautiful, charred layer on the surface while inside it is moist and succulent.

Ingredients:

- 4 T-bone steaks, about 1 inch thick
- Olive oil
- Salt and pepper
- Your favorite steak seasoning or rub

Instructions:

- They cook these on a Traeger Grill and the grills should be preheated to 450 degrees Fahrenheit. For grilling, you should consider using your preferred hardwood pellets that familiarize with grilling include oak, hickory, and mesquite.

- Use a paper towel to dry the T-bone steaks before seasoning them: 1) Lightly coat each T-bone steak with olive oil. Rinse the steaks under cold water and pat dry with paper towels When dry season the steaks with salt, pepper, and steak seasoning/rub of your choice, liberally on both sides.

- Position the seasoned T-bone steaks right on the grates of your Traeger as they are already placed on the grill. Lute the lid and chargrill for 3 to 4 minutes a side or until the steaks are at your required stage of doneness. In case you are interested in a medium-rare steak, bring the internal temperature to 130-135 degrees Fahrenheit, while in the event of a, medium steak, get a temperature of 135-145°F.

- Once the steaks are grilled to the specified doneness, transfer them away from the grill and allow to stand for some time before slicing. This causes the juices to redistribute and help the base meat to be juicy and tender in consistency.

- T-bone steaks should be sliced across the bone into thick portions, arrange steaks on a dish and treat with heat; serve with side dishes like roasted potatoes, grilled asparagus, or green vegetation. Step up your grilling game and indulge in the delicious taste and juicy chops of the T-bone steaks.

Tips:

- o T-bone steaks come with strip steaks and a thin filet, blending the juicy top cut of steak and the soft, tender meat of a tenderloin.

- o If you feel that you want more, you can season the steaks one more time with a pat of butter or fresh herbs just before serving.

- o After cooking T-bone steaks, any leftovers can be kept in a closed container for 3-4 days in the refrigerator. They are best to be eaten cold especially in salads however, they can also be warm for sandwiches, or they can be warmed in a moderate oven for some time or in microwave.

5.10 Smoked Pastrami

Serves: 10

Cooking Time: 10 hours

Temperature: 225°F

Pastrami is another lightly smoked product that has a tremendous appetite boosting smell, flavor and is perfect when cut into thin slices and used on sandwiches, salads, or just as finger food. Preparing pastrami in the Traeger Grill, ensures that the individual seasonings and smoke are controlled to taste tender juicy meat with a rich smoky flavor.

Ingredients:

- 5 lbs beef brisket, flat cut

Brine ingredients:
- 1 gallon water
- 1 cup kosher salt
- 1 cup brown sugar
- 2 tablespoons pink curing salt
- 1 tablespoon whole black peppercorns
- 1 tablespoon coriander seeds
- 1 tablespoon mustard seeds
- 1 tablespoon garlic powder
- 1 tablespoon onion powder
- 1 tablespoon paprika
- 1 teaspoon cloves

Pastrami rub ingredients:
- 2 tablespoons coarsely ground black pepper
- 2 tablespoons coriander seeds, coarsely ground
- 1 tablespoon smoked paprika
- 1 tablespoon brown sugar
- 1 teaspoon garlic powder
- 1 teaspoon onion powder

Instructions:

- In a giant stockpot, mix the water, kosher salt, brown sugar, #1 & #2 curing salt, black pepper, coriander seeds, yellow mustard seeds, garlic salt, onion salt, paprika, and ground cloves. Heat until it boils and as soon as it starts boiling get off the heat and let cool till the next day.

- Put the beef brisket in a large bowl or a resealable plastic food bag before pouring the cooled brine over the meat, ensuring the brisket is fully immersed in the solution. Place it in a refrigerator in the brine solution and allow it to sit for 5-7 days while turning it over several times for even brining.

- When done with brining, take the brisket out from the brine solution and wash it under cold water to help reduce the saltness of the meat and also to wash off any of the spices used in the solution. Season the brisket by heating 4 tablespoons of oil in a skillet set over medium-high heat and take the brisket and pat it dry with paper towels.

- On the Traeger Grill your food should be preheated at approximately 225 degrees Fahrenheit. You should use the hardwood pellets for smoking this dish and some types include the oak, hickory, and mesquite.

- To make the pastrami rub, first, put the coarsely ground black pepper, ground coriander seeds, smoked paprika, brown sugar garlic powder, and onion powder in a small bowl. Coating the mixture uniformly over the external part of the meat will do the trick; ensure that the corresponding sides are entirely covered.

- Put the seasoned brisket right on the grill grates of your Traeger as indicated in the best practices mentioned above. Shut the lid and let it smoke for about 8-10 hours or until the center of the brisket is tender and the internal temperature is 195-200°F whenever you are ready.

- Finally, when the pastrami is well cooked and browned it should be lifted from the grill and placed on a chopping boar. It has to be left for 30 minutes to an hour to permit the juices to flow to the center of the meat. I would suggest cutting the pastrami as finely as we can across the muscle fibers for optimum succulence.

- Enjoy the smoked pastrami whether it is cold or served hot as a sliced tenderloin, topped with mustard and pickles on a rye bread to form the perfect pastrami sandwich. You can also use it to prepare Reuben sandwiches, pastrami hash or else remit the same alongside sauerkraut and potatoes for a healthier meal. Now you can also relish the taste of homemade smoked pastrami that has a wonderful flavor and pleasant smell.

Tips:

- To obtain the optimum outcome, prepare a flat-cut brisket with decent layering of fat for moisture and enhanced taste in the pastrami.

- To reduce the amount of heat, you can tone down the spiciness of the pastrami rub by altering the amount of black pepper, smoked paprika, or even Chili flakes.

- In its raw state, pastrami undergoes the same curing process as other types of meat and can be cured and smoked in advance for later consumption Remaining smoked pastrami can be stored in a tightly sealed container in the refrigerator for a maximum of a week or can also be frozen. Use it like any regular BBQ sauce in sandwiches, salads, soups, or any recipe that you need a pastrami flavor for!

Chapter 6: Pork Paradise

Welcome to pork paradise, where the flavors are bold, the meat is tender, and every dish is a celebration of deliciousness. Pork is incredibly versatile, and your Traeger Grill is the perfect tool to bring out its best. In this chapter, we explore a variety of pork dishes that are sure to become favorites in your grilling repertoire.

From the juicy pulled pork shoulder that's perfect for sandwiches and tacos to the smoky delight of baby back ribs, these recipes will make your mouth water. Discover the savory goodness of grilled pork chops, the elegance of smoked ham, and the fun twist of bacon-wrapped asparagus. Each recipe is crafted to highlight the natural flavors of pork while adding a unique smoky touch. Whether you're cooking for a crowd or just for yourself, these pork recipes are designed to impress. Let's dive into the world of pork paradise and make every meal a flavorful adventure.

6.1 Pulled Pork Shoulder

Serves: 12

Cooking Time: 8-10 hours

Temperature: 225°F

Pulled pork shoulder is the epitome of a good barbecue dish and it is great for preparing a Sunday lunch or even using it for the entire week. This Low N Slow method on a Traeger Grill yields juicy meat that is ideal for sandwich, tacos, salads and more.

Ingredients:

- 8-10 lbs pork shoulder (also known as pork butt)
- Your favorite pork rub or seasoning
- Wood chips or pellets, such as apple, cherry, or hickory

Instructions:

- Temperature setting should be to 225°F for the Traeger Grill. You should make sure to use your preferred hardwood pellets to smoke your dish and this commonly comes in apple, cherry, and hickory flavors.

- You need to make sure that the pork shoulder is dry, so patting it with paper towels is necessary, and you should remove any thick layer of fat on the surface. After well trussing the meat, use your favored rub or seasoning and spread over the pork shoulder for its all sides.

- Put the seasoned pork shoulder on the grill grate of your Traeger with its fatty side facing downward on the hot surface. After that, smoke it for one and a half to two hours, or until the internal temperature hits 195-200F and the meat can be pulled easily with a fork.

- Once your pork shoulder is ready, it is important to take it off the grill carefully and then place it onto a serving tray or a chopping board. After that allow it to rest for 30-60 minutes to allow juices to drip back to the meat. Pull the pork shoulder apart with two forks or meat claws into small pieces, removing excess fat and sinews when done.

- Enjoy the pulled pork shoulder warm with a sauce of your choosing on the side or toss it in the sauce before serving, and some common side dishes for barbecued meat include coleslaw, baked beans, and cornbread. Eaten piled high on sandwiches, in tacos, over rice or mashed potatoes making it a lovely filling and tasty meal.

Tips:

- o We're cooking with pork shoulder here, and as mentioned before this type of meat is quite easy to work with in terms of timing. It is complete once they become soft and the minute, they can be separated with just the use of fingers in a shredding like manner.

- o To add even more taste to the pork shoulder, mix apple juice, cider vinegar, and preferred spices and subsequent injection into the meat before smoking.

- o The ingredients When you have leftovers of pulled pork shoulder, you can store it in an airtight container then it can be stored in the refrigerator for not more than 3-4 days and can also be frozen for longer storage. It can be eaten in sandwiches, salads, soups, or any other option that requires juicy, well-cooked pulled pork!

6.2 Grilled Pork Chops

Serves: 4

Cooking Time: 20 minutes

Temperature: 400°F

Here is an easy pork chops recipe that grills in no time at all and eliminates the tiresome task of carving big roasts or steaks. End up with moist and tasty chops that boast of an appealing char from grilling on your Traeger Grill.

Ingredients:

> ➤ 4 pork chops, about 1 inch thick
> ➤ Olive oil
> ➤ Salt and pepper
> ➤ Your favorite pork seasoning or marinade

Instructions:

- Set your Traeger Grill function to the smoke setting and preheat for 10 to 15 minutes with the lid closed at 400 degrees. If you have your preferred hardwood pellets for grilling, you may use any of the above varieties including oak, hickory, or maple.

- Dry them with paper towels and then lightly soak them with olive oil to coat! Coat the chops nicely with the seasonings and marinate of your preference which may include salt, pepper, and any preferred pork seasoning.

- To cook pork chops: put the seasoned pork chops directly on the grill grates of your Traeger. Shut the lid and cook each side for 4-5 minutes until the internal temperature of the chop has reached 145°F as So, read the temperature using a meat thermometer inserted into the thickest part of the chop.

- After the pork chops have been cooked, you need to be very careful so that you do not lose the food, and then you should put the chops on a serving dish. Let them stand for about 5 minutes before consuming to allow the juices to spread evenly across the food.

- As you prepare the perfectly grilled pork chops, make sure to serve it hot accompanied with boiled or roasted vegetables, mashed potatoes, or green salads. Read and learn on how to prepare mouthwatering juicy pork chops that are tender when you grill them on the Traeger Grill.

Tips:

- Pork chops require attention not to be overcooked; otherwise, they turn to tough and dry on the inside. Target an internal temperature of 160 degrees F to for a great tasting and tender pork chop.

- To add some more taste, it is suggested to apply your preferred sauce that you wish to marinate the pork chops at least for thirty minutes to an hour before grilling.

- Preparing grilled pork chops for the next meal is very simple; you should put the leftovers in an airtight container and store it in the refrigerator for up to 3-4 days. It is recommended to consume them cold either as a filling for the sandwich or as a topping to the salad or You can warm up the cheesy notes in low heat then serve it.

6.3 Smoked Baby Back Ribs

Serves: 6

Cooking Time: 5-6 hours

Temperature: 225°F

BBQ Smoked baby back Ribs are favorites all over the barbecuing arena because of their tender meat and delicious taste. When cooked slowly on the Traeger Grill, the meat acquires tenderness that is falling off the bone and is laden with mouthwatering smokiness.

Ingredients:

- 2 racks baby back ribs
- Your favorite rib rub or seasoning
- Wood chips or pellets, such as hickory, apple, or pecan
- Barbecue sauce (optional, for serving)

Instructions:

- Tear the large ingredients into smaller ones and preheat the Traeger Grill to 225°F. It is advisable to utilize the favored hardwood pellets for smoking purposes comprised of hickory, apple, or pecan pellets.

- Place ribs on a cutting board with the bony side facing up and then using a butter knife lift membrane on the back of the ribs while using a paper towel to trap and lift the membrane. Discard the surface drained from the water and wipe the ribs dry with paper towel afterwards spread your preferred rib rub spice or season over the ribs making sure every part is covered.

- Arrange the ribs brushed with the seasoning on the grill grates of your Traeger, with the bone side facing down. Shut the lid and smoke for 5-6 hours, or until the meat becomes tender and detaches from the bones.

- Following the above directions, if you wish, ascend to the last 30 minutes, glaze the ribs with your preferred BBQ sauce. They will require close supervision to avoid making them burnt.

- When the ribs have been thoroughly cooked on the grill, you should remove them from the heat and place it on a chopping board. For the sauce, prepare the BBQ sauce by heating the olive oil in the pan, then adding the garlic and sauté for about two minutes.
- Do not sever the ribs at the bone; instead, lay them flat and cut in between them to form individual ribs.

- To elaborate smoked baby back ribs, you should present them hot with extra servings of the barbecue sauce of your choice served on the side and with complementing meals such as coleslaw, baked beans, and cornbread. This Traeger Grill recipe allows you to indulge in juicy, tasty meat and have the scent of smoke in a flash!

Tips:

- For added flare, you can soak the ribs in a mixture of Apple juice, cider vinegar and your choice of spices for a few hours before proceeding with the smoking method.

- To determine readiness for serving, quite often you see a crust on them, like bark and then you see that the meat is tender and easily comes off the bones.

- From the above details, it implies that leftover smoked baby back ribs can be kept in a sealed container and can also be stored in a fridge for up to 3-4 days. Before you serve them again, warm them up in a stove or microwave and taste the deliciousness over and over!

6.4 Grilled Pork Tenderloin

Serves: 4

Cooking Time: 30 minutes

Temperature: 375°F

Grilled pork tenderloin is versatile, delicious, and tender muscle that cook quickly, it best served for weeknight meals and festive occasions. Preparing it on your Traeger Grill makes it tastier and softer with that rich smoky feel to the pork meat.

Ingredients:

- ➤ 2 pork tenderloins, about 1 pound each
- ➤ Olive oil
- ➤ Salt and pepper
- ➤ Your favorite pork seasoning or marinade

Instructions:

- Prepare your Traeger Grill to medium high heat which corresponds to about 375 degrees Fahrenheit. For the grilling process, remember always to use your preferred hardwood pellets, which include maple, cherry, and pecan.

- Take the pork tenderloins and just dry the skin on them and season with olive oil so that it can coat the skin. Coat the tenderloins well with salt, pepper, and any chosen pork-seasoning/marinade on all faces.

- Lay the seasoned pork tenderloins right on the grill grate of your Traeger without putting them on the cast iron grate. Shut and grill for about 15-20 mins, flipping a few times to brown, or until the internal temperature is about 145°F, if using a meat thermometer in the middle of the tenderloin.

- After preparing the pork tenderloins, it is important to carefully make sure they are removed from the grill and best served on a chopping board. Allow them to relax a bit before carving into thick steaks.

- This grilled pork tenderloin is best served immediately; however, if for some reason you can't, you can safely reheat before serving with your preferred side dishes like roasted veggies, rice, or greens. This must-have steak recipe will allow you to taste the juicy meat and feel the smoky taste of coal from the Traeger Grill.

Tips:

- ○ Pork tenderloin does not take long to cook, well done, and therefore, should be checked frequently to avoid them becoming well-done.

- ○ For even more taste and as a further recommendation, you can marinate the pork tenderloin in your preferred marinade so that it can be grilled for about 30 minutes to 1 hour.

- ○ In fact, to retain the juicy of the pork meat, leftover grilled pork tenderloin should be stored in an airtight container and consume within 3-4 days of grilling. it is particularly tasty served cold and ideal for sandwiches, salads or even just eaten on its own but, can also be warmed gently in the oven or microwave and served.

6.5 Smoked Ham

Serves: 10

Cooking Time: 4 hours

Temperature: 225°F

Smoked ham to be specific is one of my most preferred meals and is often prepared during festive seasons, either Easter, Christmas, or any other occasion that one feels like having some good meal. This recipe shows you how to prepare a delicious ham using an electric Traeger Grill which will give you juicy results and tasteful flavors.

Ingredients:

> ➢ 1 bone-in ham, preferably spiral-cut (about 8-10 pounds)
> ➢ Your favorite ham glaze or seasoning
> ➢ Wood chips or pellets, such as apple or cherry

Instructions:

- Before starting cooking, the Traeger Grill should be preheated to 225 degrees Fahrenheit. Smoking recommendation: use your favorite hardwood pellets for smoking, for instance, apple pellets, cherry pellets, etc.

- Take out the ham from its packaging and put it on a large foil of aluminum foil to be tenderize. If this is so preferred, the surface of the ham must be scored in a diamond form using a sharp knife to allow for easier penetration of the glaze.

- You can glaze the ham and cook it in various methods. Season the ham and brush it with your preferred ham glaze before cooking, on all sides. There are also options of sweet glazes as the honey or maple syrup glaze or savory glazes as the mustard brown sugar.

- Once done, it's best to place the glazed ham directly on the grates of your

Traeger or keep it on the foil for convenience in cleaning up. Shut the lid and smoke for 3-4 hours, or until the middle of the ham – cooked to 140°F) as measured with a meat thermometer.

- If so desired, pour over the make use of the leftover glaze or some of the juices in the foil to baste the ham every one to two hours.

- If you are using a charcoal grill, once the ham is done, using care, move the ham away from the heat, over to a serving dish. It is only important to slice it thinly then serve when ready to be eaten, after letting it rest a few minutes.

- Enjoy the smoked ham warm or at the temperature of a room with other recipes that include grilled potatoes, beans, or any type of vegetables. Why not cook smoked ham using the correct recipe from the Traeger Grill and enjoy the smoky taste and tender feel of the food.

Tips:

- When I used a ham that is pre-spiral cut, be careful when covering it since using foil will make it take long to smoke; many hours that it will dry up.

- You can add cinnamon, adjust the amount of honey, or use other types of it, and modify the other ingredients to your liking.

- Smoked ham can be homemade or bought at the market; the leftovers should be wrapped well and placed in an airtight container and stored in the fridge for 3-4 days. Better still, serve it cold in sandwiches, salads or in soups, but if you prefer it hot, warm it slowly in the oven or using a microwave Serve it cold in sandwiches, salads and soups or reheat it gently in the oven or microwave and serve warm.

6.6 Grilled Bacon-Wrapped Asparagus

Serves: 6

Cooking Time: 25 minutes

Temperature: 375°F

Bacon must wrap and marinated asparagus is sure to be a hit as an appetizer or side dish as it has a hint of smoky bacon crisps with the fresh, firm asparagus. This is because cooking the asparagus on your Traeger Grill enhances the flavors, while the method help you prepare the best asparagus.

Ingredients:

> ➢ 1 pound fresh asparagus spears, trimmed
> ➢ 12 slices bacon
> ➢ Olive oil
> ➢ Salt and pepper
> ➢ Toothpicks

Instructions:

- First, it is essential to heat your Traeger Grill with the temperature of about 375°F. So, you need to make sure that what is going into your grill is your preferred hardwood pellets like maple or pecan.

- Asparagus:
- Rinse the asparagus spears and cut off the stalk ends where they are woody. Right before placing them in the oven, pour a little olive oil over the okra and sprinkle some salt and pepper on a plate.

- Take 4-5 asparagus and tie them along with each other and then wrap them along with a slice of bacon from one end and layer it around till you reach the asparagus tips. Sprinkle the remaining cocktail sauce over the bacon. Place the pieces of bacon onto the prepared baking sheet and secure both ends with toothpicks.

- Arrange the bacon-wrapped asparagus bundles right on the grill grates in your Traeger, with the layer of bacon evenly facing down. You will need to shut the lid and grill for 20-25 minutes, flipping the bacon occasionally, until it is crunchy, and the asparagus is soft.

- When you start getting the bacon-wrapped asparagus ready, make sure you take them off the grill and place them on a dish gently. Serve them hot as a starter or even as an accompaniment to snacked served with your favorite meal.

Tips:

- ○ Should you desire for some added zing, you can always top the bacon-wrapped asparagus bundles with garnishes such as grated Parmesan cheese or coat the bundles in balsamic glaze.

- It is recommended to pre-soak wooden toothpicks 30 minutes in warm water before cooking to avoid candle-like ignition on a grill.

- After grilling, the bacon-wrapped asparagus can be covered and kept in the refrigerator for a couple of days for consumption the next day. These fillets may be served cold, or they can be reheated gently in the oven or even in microwave.

6.7 Smoked Sausage Links

Serves: 6

Cooking Time: 1 hour

Temperature: 225°F

Smoked sausage links are also a very satisfactory meal if served on their own as a carnivorous meal, chopped and included in some pasta sauces or soup or included in an appetizer list to be served with crackers and cheese. Preparing them on your Traeger Grill makes it smoky is very important in making the sausage juicy and full of flavors each time.

Ingredients:

- 2 pounds smoked sausage links, such as kielbasa, bratwurst, or Italian sausage
- Your favorite barbecue sauce or mustard (optional, for serving)

Instructions:

- Turn the Traeger Grill On and set the temperature to 225 degrees Fahrenheit. It is recommended you use the hardwood pellets that you prefer most for smoking, this includes hickory, apple, and mesquite.

- put the smoked sausage links directly on the grill grates of your Traeger as illustrated below. Close the lid and smoke for 45-60 minutes or until the internal temperature is around 160°F when using meat thermometer skewered into the thickest portion of the sausage.

- For those who prefer such toppings, during the final 10-15 minutes of grilling, baste the sausage links with the barbecue sauce or mustard of your choice for extra flavor and for a nice caramelization.

- It is when the sausage links are cooked on one side, you start to carefully lift them from the grill to a serving plate. Present it hot with extra barbecue sauce or mustard served alongside the dish, if preferred.

Tips:

- As for the smoked sausage links that you could use for the preparation of this recipe, you may opt for kielbasa, bratwurst, chorizo, or Italian sausage. Pick your flavor of choice or decide to switch between two different filing choices.

- Always pierce the sausage links once you are done with the preparation to create a number of holes using a fork of knife before you smoke since this is useful in ensuring that the sausage fat melts, and the sausage does not burn in the smoker.

- Frozen smoked sausage links should be placed in a new airtight container, and they can be put in the refrigerator and will last for 3-4 days. This way you can serve them cold sliced with sandwiches or cold dishes or warm slightly with the help of oven or microwave – to your table.

6.8 Grilled Pork Belly

Serves: 4

Cooking Time: 2 hours

Temperature: 300°F

Pork belly barbeque is one delicious entrée that is best for lovers of juicy and tasty food since it is creamy and will satisfy your cravings for pork meat. Through sous vide preparation, the muscular, marbled pork belly gets tender when cooked on your Traeger Grill, while the surface of the skin develops the Maillard reaction from grilling on high heat.

Ingredients:

- 2 pounds pork belly, skin-on
- Salt and pepper
- Your favorite pork seasoning or marinade

Instructions:

- First, set your Traeger Grill on the highest smoke setting and let the grill heat up to around 300 degrees F. While grilling, we recommend your preferred hardwood pellets: oak or cherry.

- It is worthy to note that for better and evenly crisped rind, one should pat the pork belly dry with paper towel and then score the skin with a sharp knife, about 1/4 inch deep, creating square like patterns all over the rind surface. Rinse the pork belly and dab with paper towels to dry Season with salt, pepper, and your preferred pork seasoning or rub on both sides of the meat.

- Arrange the seasoned pork belly without the tray on the grill of your Traeger, with its skin facing upwards. Turn the grill on and close the lid Place on the grill and allow to cook for 1. 5-2 hours or when the meat of the pork belly is so tender that a fork can easily penetrate, and the meat thermometer reads 200°F when inserted in the thickest part of the pork belly.

- Depending on the crispiness you desire for the skin, if it is not crispy enough towards the end of cooking, the Traeger Grill can be elevated to 400°F and the chicken can be grilled for an additional 10-15 minutes, but keep a close eye on it to avoid any burning.

- When preparing the pork belly ensure that it reaches to juicy and tender state then take a lot of caution while transferring from the grill to a cutting board. Allow it to cool for a few minutes after the steaming process before cutting it into thick slices or cubes.

- Enjoy the grilled pork belly while it's still sizzling, with steamed white rice, some stir-fried vegetables or a crisp salad. Savor the vigor of your fish skin and tenderness of the meat through the freshly Grilled Fish on Traeger!

Tips:

- To enhance the taste, you can season the pork belly with your preferred marinade and allow the meat to past through the marinade for some hours before barbecuing.

- What is, however, important is that leftover grilled pork belly should be kept in the refrigerator, in an airtight jar, where it should remain fresh for 3-4 days. On the third day, bake again in a low heat oven or warming it in the microwave and use it to eat again and again.

6.9 Smoked Pork Loin

Serves: 6

Cooking Time: 2. 5 hours

Temperature: 225°F

Other popular vegetables include the pork loin that is normally prepared as a barbecue meal to feed many people at once. This should be cooked slow on your Traeger Grill to give it tenderness and juicy meat with a theme smoky touch that everybody will crave.

Ingredients:

> - 1 pork loin roast, about 3-4 pounds
> - Olive oil
> - Salt and pepper
> - Your favorite pork seasoning or rub

Instructions:

- First, preheat your Traeger Grill for about five minutes until its temperature reaches 225 degrees Fahrenheit. Hardwood pellets can be utilized for smoking, but smokers should be careful with hickory, apple, and cherry pellets.

- In a separate large mixing bowl, mix the salt, sugar, onion and garlic powders, and black pepper with 2 tablespoons of olive oil and rub this mixture over the surface of the pork loin roast, patting it dry with a paper towel first. Coat the broiler pork liberally with salt, pepper, and the desired pork seasoning or pork rub, including the sides.

- Position the seasoned pork loin in the middle of the surface of the grill without placing it in the wire grate, with the fatty side facing upwards. Shut the lid and continue smoking for about 2 – 3 hours, or when the internal temperature containing a meat thermometer is between 63-68°C when inserted into the at the thickest part of the pork loin.

- Once you are sure that your pork loin is well cooked cover it and take it out of the grill to the chopping board. Allow it to cool for a few minutes; then, cut it into thick pieces that can be eaten together with the juice.

- The smoked pork loin is perfectly suitable to be served hot as a main course along with any side dish of your liking, for instance mashed potatoes, roasted veggies, or a crisp green salad. Savor the tastiness and moist trajectory of grilled delicacies from the Traeger Grill!

Tips:

- For added taste, you can marinate the pork loin in water, salt, sugar, and other spices then allow it to soak in the prepared mixture for several hours before smoking.

- Cold-smoked pork loin can also be kept in the refrigerator in an airtight container for about 3 to 4 days. It can be stored in an airtight container for up to a day, after heating gently in the oven or microwave, it can be eaten again and again.

6.10 Grilled BBQ Ribs

Serves: 6

Cooking Time: 5 hours

Temperature: 225°F

As one of the all-time favorite barbeque specialties, an easy to prepare and deliciously grilled BBQ ribs is something best enjoyed during celebrations or any occasion even just for those random moments when you get to craving for the soft, juicy meat with a savory sweet sauce. Helps to cook the ribs low and slow on the Traeger grill to make them tender, succulent, and possess a rich smoky taste that everyone will enjoy.

Ingredients:

- 2 racks pork spareribs or baby back ribs
- Your favorite rib rub or seasoning
- Your favorite barbecue sauce
- Wood chips or pellets, such as hickory, apple, or cherry

Instructions:

- And thus, prepare your Traeger Grill for cooking at 225, to achieve the best out of the dish or meal you are preparing. Smoke it using your favorite hardwood and some recommendations are hickory, apple, or cherry pellets.

- For those who are not familiar with preparing ribs, follow these steps: First, take out the membrane on the back by inserting a butter knife under the membrane and use the flat part of a paper towel to grab the membrane and pull it off. Remove any loose surface layer of fat and pat the ribs dry with paper towel Then apply your preferred rib rub & seasoning, liberally, on both sides.

- Sprinkle the ribs with your chosen seasoning and then lower them directly on the grilling grates of your Traeger, with the bones facing down. Shut the lid and smoke for about three hours while generously spraying them with apple juice or cider vinegar every one hour to avoid them getting dry.

- Finally, after 3 hours of smoking, take out the ribs from the same grill and wrap them securely in aluminum foil with the meat side uppermost. Place them back on the grill racks and cook for an additional 1. 5-2 hours or until the meat will easily pull away from the bones when done.

- Take the ribs out from the foil and spread your preferred barbecue sauce on each of the ribs generously. Send them back to the grill and place them back for another 30 minutes so that the sauce forms on the outside would be glossy and sticky.

- When the ribs are ready, use a sharp knife or metal spatula to cut them off the grill and placed on a cutting board. Allow them to stand for a couple of minutes before slicing them along the bones to make single rib portions.

- You need to serve the grilled BBQ ribs immediately and extra barbecue sauce for those who may want to add more. Why not soak up the juicy and succulent taste of the meat and the glossy, caramelized coating from the Traeger Grill!

Tips:

- Another method of preparing the ribs is by placing it in your preferred barbecue sauce or dry rub, covering it and refrigerating for several hours or overnight prior to the smoking process.

- For another kick, optionally, you can replace the sugar with cayenne pepper or hot sauce in the barbecue sauce before pouring the glaze over the ribs.

- If there are any grilled BBQ ribs remaining it is okay to store it in a sealed container in the refrigerator and consume it within 3-4 days. They can be stored and frozen to be used later when you just warm them in the oven or the microwave to have them again.

Chapter 7: Seafood Specialties

Dive into the ocean of flavors with our seafood specialties, bringing the best of the sea to your Traeger Grill. Seafood on the grill is a culinary delight, offering a unique blend of smokiness and freshness that's hard to resist. This chapter is your guide to mastering the art of grilling and smoking seafood, turning simple ingredients into gourmet dishes.

Imagine grilling tender calamari with a hint of char, smoking lobster tails to perfection, or preparing a grilled tuna steak that melts in your mouth. We've got a variety of recipes that cover everything from shrimp skewers to smoked trout, ensuring there's something for every seafood lover.

Each recipe is designed to enhance the natural flavors of the seafood while adding a delicious smoky twist. Whether you're a seasoned seafood aficionado or just starting out, these dishes will elevate your grilling game and bring a taste of the ocean to your table.

7.1 Grilled Calamari

Serves: 4

Cooking Time: 10 minutes

Temperature: 400°F

Grilled calamari are easy to prepare and quickly can impress guests with delicate, bittersweet taste of squids. Great for those times when you want something lighter than a main course, but yet is the best way of preparing in seafood.

Ingredients:

- 1 pound calamari, cleaned and cut into rings
- 2 tablespoons olive oil
- 2 cloves garlic, minced
- Juice of 1 lemon
- Salt and pepper to taste
- Fresh parsley, chopped, for garnish

Instructions:

- First, turn on Traeger Grill to medium-high heat; it will be around 400 degrees Fahrenheit on the surface.

- Mix in a bowl Combined the calamari rings, olive oil, minced garlic lemon juice, salt, and pepper.

- Arrange the calamari rings in a straight manner on the grates or if using basket so that they do not slip through.

- Cook the calamari over the direct heat for approximately 10 minutes or until the squid changes color and turns slightly brownish.

- When it is well cooked, the shaslik should be transferred from the grill to a serving plate.

- Arrange the chopped fresh parsley on top of the preparation and serve the dish as soon as possible. Savor calamari that have been freshly cooked that is tender which has been grilled slightly to add smoky flavor to it.

Tips:

- ○ It is recommended that you drizzle the calamari with the olive oil mixture and let it marinate for about 15-30 minutes before grilling as it adds to the taste.

- ○ Best served and accompanied by a small portion of grilled vegetables or a crisp salad.

- ○ It is important to avoid ruining the preparation by overcooking the calamari since it will become firm and chewy.

7.2 Grilled Shrimp Skewers

Serves: 4

Cooking Time: 10 minutes

Temperature: 400°F

Grilled shrimp skewer is a delicious dish which is very fitting to be served during any occasion because of its ease in preparation. The shrimp are delicate, and they can be cooked for a relatively short period of time, simultaneously acquiring the magnificent taste of your marinade.

Ingredients:

- ➢ 1 pound large shrimp, peeled and deveined
- ➢ 2 tablespoons olive oil
- ➢ 2 cloves garlic, minced
- ➢ Juice of 1 lemon
- ➢ Salt and pepper to taste
- ➢ Fresh parsley, chopped, for garnish
- ➢ Wooden or metal skewers

Instructions:

- Prepare your Traeger Grill to 400 degrees Fahrenheit so that the cobbler can be cooked at the right temperature.

- Using a bowl, blend the shrimp with olive oil, minced garlic, juice of a lemon, salt, and pepper.

- Regarding preparation order for the shrimp, four proposed steps include threading the shrimp onto skewers.

- Texture: We also slip them easily on the grill and place them directly on the grill grates.

- Cooks the shrimp for approximately ten minutes flipping them over in the middle until their color changes to pink from white and their texture is no longer clear.

- Take out from the grill, then served immediately in a serving plate.

- Sprinkle over chopped parsley and serve. For the shrimp skewers make sure to savor this dish due to its juicy meaty shrimps that are full of flavor.

Tips:

- Adjust the wooden skewer used in grilling by soaking it in water for 30 minutes to avoid it burning out.

- For another course, eat with rice, a plate of grilled vegetables, or a delicious salad for the ideal meal.

- You could season the shrimp in the olive oil mixture and allow it to rest for 15-30 minutes before grilling.

7.3 Smoked Lobster Tails

Serves: 4

Cooking Time: 45 minutes

Temperature: 225°F

This recipe is a member of the lobster family and appears to be the kind of food that adds an elegant touch of smoked flavor to the natural sweetness of the lobster. Ideal for celebratory meals or any time that you fancy indulging yourself with homeliness in a rich gourmet fashion.

Ingredients:

- 4 lobster tails
- 4 tablespoons butter, melted
- 2 cloves garlic, minced
- Juice of 1 lemon
- Salt and pepper to taste
- Fresh parsley, chopped, for garnish
- Lemon wedges for serving

Instructions:

- Thus, it is significant to preheat your Traeger Grill to a temperature of 225 degrees Fahrenheit.

- With the use of kitchen shears, remove the hard shell at the back part of the lobster tails and separate the shell by a little bit to give room for the actual lobster meat that's inside it.

- Combine the melted butter with minced garlic, lemon juice, salt, and pepper in a bowl that has just been washed.

- Coat the lobster meat Ritch-to well with the butter mixture.

- Then, place the lobster tails directly on the grill grates so that they do not lose their flavors through the grill mesh.

- Cook the lobster tails about 45 minutes with smoke, or until the meat is completely white and the insert stick will read 145 F.

- Take it out from the grill and place it onto a platter that is meant for serving.

- Beautiful garnished with chopped fresh parsley and served immediately accompanied with lemon wedges. Bamboo smoked lobster tails will provide the best experience of the smoky taste.

Tips:

- To add even more taste in the dish, pepper dust the lobster meat slightly, and put it to smoke.

- You can best accompany it with a garlic butter for dipping or even roll it into the butter before serving, for an extra luxurious experience, and a side of fresh green salad.

- ○ Consult a meat thermometer to avoid overcooking the lobster tails.

7.4 Grilled Tuna Steaks

Serves: 4

Cooking Time: 10 minutes

Temperature: 400°F

Grilled tuna steaks are a wonderful option for a hearty meal that does not skimp on taste, which is not difficult to prepare. The fact that the grill is very hot makes the outside layer of the tuna crisp while the interior section remains juicy.

Ingredients:

- ➢ 4 lobster tails
- ➢ 4 tablespoons butter, melted
- ➢ 2 cloves garlic, minced
- ➢ Juice of 1 lemon
- ➢ Salt and pepper to taste
- ➢ Fresh parsley, chopped, for garnish
- ➢ Lemon wedges for serving

Instructions:

- To do this, make sure your Traeger Grill is preheated before grilling the burgers, set the temperature to 400°F.

- Treat the tuna with little olive oil and put in the minced garlic, lemon juice, and lastly salt and pepper.

- Exercise care into portions that are best for grilling and arrange the tuna steaks directly on the grill grates.

- Barbecue the tuna piece uniformly for about 10 minutes turning on the other side once you feel that the tuna is ready to your preferred doneness.

- Let it to cook for some time until it is brown on one side, then take the food off the grill and put it on a plate for serving.

- And finally, garnish it with freshly chopped parsley to make it more appealing and then serve immediately. Take your time to taste the satisfaction brought on by the tenderness of grilled tuna steaks.

Tips:

- Truly requite a perfectly seared tuna steak follow a few techniques: Preheat the grill to a high heat and let it get hot before placing the tuna on the grill.

- Pair it with grilled vegetables or a simple greens salad to have it together and complement each other.

- If, on the other hand, you feel that the tuna should be 'rare,' you can reduce the cooking time to 5 minutes.

7.5 Smoked Oysters

Serves: 6

Cooking Time: 30 minutes

Temperature: 225°F

Smoked oysters are tender and tasty, having a mouth-popping, savory flavor that makes it ideal for appetizer or any dish as an extra item. Smoking brings in more rich taste to them and steep up the natural-salted taste of oysters.

Ingredients:

- 4 lobster tails
- 4 tablespoons butter, melted
- 2 cloves garlic, minced
- Juice of 1 lemon
- Salt and pepper to taste
- Fresh parsley, chopped, for garnish
- Lemon wedges for serving

Instructions:

- Select your heat to a low temperature, 225 degrees Fahrenheit should suffice on your Traeger Grill.

- Carefully transfer the shucked oysters to a baking sheet that is safe for grilling.

- In a bowl, take the butter and melt it over low heat, once melted add in the minced garlic and lemon juice.

- Take the butter mixture and gently paint on each oyster shell.

- Grill the oysters for about 30 mins to get the best results; this allows the flesh to cook well while absorbing the smoky flavor.

- Take it off the grill working bowl and put it on a serving dish.

- Finally, grace with fresh parsley and serve hot with lemon slices. Indulge with the smoked oysters and taste their uniqueness is because of the rich smoky flavor.

Tips:

- You can use hardwood pellets that are derived from apple or cherry wood to give you a sweet smoky flavor.

- It can be enjoyed this way while serving it alongside a glass crackers or crusty bread makes it a perfect appetizer.

- However, if this is something you really want to do, you may include a pinch of hot sauce on top before smoking or a fraction of grated Parmesan cheese.

7.6 Grilled Scallops

Serves: 4

Cooking Time: 15 minutes

Temperature: 375°F

This is a very swift dish, tasty and tender, which can be served on any event. The best and most desirable side of grilling is that scallops are cooked with a high heat, which provides the outer crust of the dish while retaining the tenderness on the inside.

Ingredients:

- ➤ 1 pound large sea scallops
- ➤ 2 tablespoons olive oil
- ➤ 2 cloves garlic, minced
- ➤ Juice of 1 lemon
- ➤ Salt and pepper to taste
- ➤ Fresh parsley, chopped, for garnish

Instructions:

- Turn preheat to 375°F on your Traeger Grill.

- Open the package of scallops and pat it dry on one side with the help of a paper towel.

- Scallops – coat the scallops with olive oil and next add minced garlic, lemon juice, and season the scallops with salt and pepper.

- Grill the scallops without any of the lid, so they sit on the grill grate.

- Cook the scallops for the next 15 minutes turning one side and ensuring that they have change color from translucent to white with some dark brown, charred crusts on the outside.

- Take out and serve on a dish that may be placed on a serving table or a side table.

- Sprinkle the chopped fresh parsley over the servings then serve immediately to allow the juice to settle. Savor and feel the taste of scallop, sweet, tender that has been grilled for the best consumption.

Tips:

- o After defrosting the scallops, try to pat them as dry as possible so that when the grilling is being done you get that good sear.

- o It still needs a side dish, and my suggestion is boiled or roasted vegetables or even a simple green salad.

- o To add more depth of the flavors you can baste the scallops in the olive oil mixture and then grill for extra 15 to 30 minutes.

7.7 Smoked Mahi Mahi

Serves: 4

Cooking Time: 1 hour

Temperature: 225°F

I love smoked mahi mahi and it goes well as a seafood recipe especially when prepared during the summer season. Smoking complements the inherent taste of the fish by giving it a subtle smoky flavor, rounded sweetness which is mildly sweet in the mouth.

Ingredients:

- 4 mahi mahi fillets
- 2 tablespoons olive oil
- 2 cloves garlic, minced
- Juice of 1 lime
- Salt and pepper to taste
- Fresh cilantro, chopped, for garnish

Instructions:

- First, set your Traeger Grill to the desired level of cooking by setting it to 225°F or medium heat.

- Marinate the mahi mahi fillets with olive oil and sprinkle with garlic, lime juice, salt a d black pepper.

- This is because placing the fillets directly on the grill grates will avoid unnecessary soaking of the fish in oil while grilling.

- Prepare the mahi mahi by placing on the grill and cooking for about an hour, or until the fish is soft, and reaches the required temperature of up to 145°F.

- As soon as those are grilled to your preference, carefully place the chicken from the grill to the serving platter.

- Proceed to garnishing the rice with finely chopped fresh cilantro before serving immediately. Marvel at the subtle, grilled jerkiness of the scrumptious smoked mahi mahi.

Tips:

- For a milder and sweeter taste, Preferred fruitwood pellets are apple or cherry flavors with fish.

- The popular recipe pairs well with a plate of grilled vegetables or a dish of salsa and citrus for a colorful dish.

- If you wish to have a more potent smoky taste, you might make a brine solution containing water, salt, and sugar and let the mahi mahi sit in it for about an hour or just over two hours.

7.8 Grilled Clams

Serves: 4

Cooking Time: 20 minutes

Temperature: 375°F

Clams grilled are delicious appetizers that do not require a lot of preparation and cooking time to prepare well while still retaining their delicious natural flavor. Ideal for the beginning of the meal or as a dedicated dish, they will certainly not leave guests indifferent.

Ingredients:

- 2 dozen fresh clams
- 2 tablespoons olive oil
- 2 cloves garlic, minced
- Juice of 1 lemon
- Salt and pepper to taste
- Fresh parsley, chopped, for garnish
- Lemon wedges for serving

Instructions:

- In instances where the Traeger Grill instructions call for 'Moderate Heat,' you should ensure that the Grill is preheated at around 375 degrees Fahrenheit.

- To prepare the poaching liquid, in a bowl mix the clams with olive oil, minced garlic, lemon juice, salt and pepper.

- Location of the clams on the grill grates offers ease of grilling and using a grill basket if at all the clams are small.

- Cook the clams for approximately 20 minutes over grill to check when they open and cook completely.

- When prepared for adequate amounts of time, it should be taken off the grill and placed on the serving platter.

- Sprinkle the chopped fresh parsley on top and immediately serve the soup with lemon wedges or slices. Savor the rich taste of the food that is ready to be savored through grilling process clams.

Tips:

- o If any clams have not opened during the grilling process, avoid eating them.

- o It is best served as a main dish accompanied with buttered garlic toast, so you can sop up all the yummy drippings.

- o To make it even more delicious, one will add water and a glass or two of white wine to the clams before grilling.

7.9 Smoked Trout

Serves: 4

Cooking Time: 2 hours

Temperature: 225°F

One of the fish preparations that are quite delicious and nutritious are smoked trout food preparation is good for any meal occasion. Smoking involves covering the trout in smoke to absorb the smoky flavor that complements its sweetness.

Ingredients:

- ➢ 4 whole trout, cleaned and gutted
- ➢ 2 tablespoons olive oil

- ➢ 2 cloves garlic, minced
- ➢ Juice of 1 lemon
- ➢ Salt and pepper to taste
- ➢ Fresh dill, chopped, for garnish
- ➢ Lemon wedges for serving

Instructions:

- Make sure your Traeger Grill is suited to 225°F before starting with the barbecue process.

- Preheat the oven and prepare the trout by brushing it with olive oil then marinating it with minced garlic, lemon juice, salt, and pepper.

- Put the trout right on the grate or the bar that you use for the fish.

- Prepare for smoking by preheating the grill, and then place trout on the grill for approximately two hours until the fish is tender and the temperature inside the fish reaches 145°F.

- The steak is now ready to be served after it has been grilled, take it off the grill and place it on a serving plate.

- In a small bowl, combine chopped fresh dill and sprinkle over the top of the potatoes; serve at once with lemon wedges. Savor smoked trout – truly unique with its warm, peaty hue.

Tips:

- o When using hardwoods, you're better of going for alder or oak woods to give your food a smoky flavor.

- o This dish, while being flavorful and hearty, should be accompanied by a side of roasted vegetables or a simple green salad for a more complete meal.

- o However, if you would like smokier flavor to the trout, you can soak it in the strong brine of water, salt, and sugar for 1-2 hours before smoking it.

7.10 Smoked Crab Legs

Serves: 4

Cooking Time: 1 hour

Temperature: 225°F

Preparing smoked crab legs is quite simple and delicious, plus, it can be considered a gourmet delicacy that is best for celebrations. Smoking slightly brings the smoky flavor in addition to the natural sugars present in the crab meat.

Ingredients:

- ➢ 4 pounds crab legs
- ➢ 4 tablespoons butter, melted
- ➢ 2 cloves garlic, minced
- ➢ Juice of 1 lemon
- ➢ Fresh parsley, chopped, for garnish
- ➢ Lemon wedges for serving

Instructions:

- Adjust your Traeger Grill to reach 225-degrees Fahrenheit prior to cooking your food items.

- Take another bowl and combine the melted butter with the minced garlic and lemon juice in it and toss until it becomes smooth.

- Rinse the crab legs with warm water and then pat dry using a paper towel; coat the crab legs with butter and then rub using the remaining butter mixture.

- Position the crab legs in such a way that they are placed directly onto the grill grates.

- To prepare the crab legs for smoking, prepare a smoker and fill it with apple and hickory woods, which add a touch of sweetness and smoke to foods that are being smoked.

- When fully cooked, take the fillet from the grill and place it on a separate serving dish.

- Adults may take a teaspoon of lemon juice and sprinkle some chopped parsley on top before consuming Let it PS: It's best served hot with lemon wedges. experience the delectable and delicious taste of smoked crab legs.

Tips:

- o Either fruitwood nice and mild with a hint of sweetness, about like an apple or cherry for example, which blend well with the catch.

- o To keep it uncomplicated, it should be served with butter that has been melted and poured over it before being accompanied by green vegetables for what can be regarded as an ideal meal.

- o Speaking of crab legs, if you wish, before making the smoking process, you can steam it for a few minutes to enhance the tenderness.

Chapter 8: Vegetarian Delights

Vegetarians, rejoice! This chapter is dedicated to you, showcasing the amazing potential of grilled and smoked vegetables. With the Traeger Grill, you can create vegetarian dishes that are bursting with flavor, offering a smoky, savory experience that's anything but boring.

From hearty grilled portobello mushrooms that make a perfect main dish to the colorful and nutritious grilled vegetable skewers, these recipes are designed to please vegetarians and meat-lovers alike. Discover the deliciousness of smoked stuffed peppers, the comfort of smoked mac and cheese, and the elegance of grilled asparagus with a zesty lemon twist.

Each recipe is crafted to bring out the best in vegetables, using the grill to add depth and complexity to their natural flavors. Let's transform your vegetarian meals into culinary masterpieces that everyone will love.

8.1 Grilled Portobello Mushrooms

Serves: 4

Cooking Time: 20 minutes

Temperature: 375°F

One of my favorite grilling recipes is for portobello mushrooms: They are both tasty and filling, good enough for a main course or a side dish. These vegetables have a firm and dense structures, and their taste is quite intense and filling, with some of the strongest busts being the favorite forms of foods for vegetarians and non – vegetarians.

Ingredients:

> - 4 large portobello mushrooms, stems removed
> - 3 tablespoons olive oil
> - 2 cloves garlic, minced
> - 1 tablespoon balsamic vinegar
> - Salt and pepper to taste
> - Fresh parsley, chopped, for garnish

Instructions:

- It is recommended that you do this and preheat the Traeger Grill to 375 degrees Fahrenheit.

- garlic, balsamic vinegar, salt, and pepper – in a small bowl, whisk and combine the olive oil.

- Coat the portobello mushrooms evenly with the olive oil mix Spread the olive oil mixture over the mushrooms.

- Grill the mushrooms gill-side up without using any grilling accessories such as grill pans, woks, or baking sheets.

- Grill for approximately ten minutes on one side, before flipping the steaks and grilling for another ten minutes on the other side or until tender and succulent.

- Slap off from the grill and arrange in a serving platter. It is important as it enables me to remove the fowl from the grill so it can be served to the consumers.

- This meal is best served hot so take it off the heat, garnish with chopped fresh parsley and serve immediately. It was grilled even more delicious than before when penetrated the meaty flavor of portobello mushrooms.

Tips:

- o Paneer marinated in spices can be enjoyed with side orders of grilled vegetables or can be topped on a toasted bun to make a delectable mushroom burger.

- o To boost the chance of absorbing the seasoning improve the flavor, the mushrooms should be marinated in the olive oil mixture for 30minutes before grilling.

- o If you want to be more adventures and make it more flavorful, you can put a slice of your desired cheese over the mushrooms about five to seven minutes before you are done grilling.

8.2 Smoked Stuffed Peppers

Serves: 4

Cooking Time: 1 hour

Temperature: 350°F

Stuffed peppers in particular smoked pepper is very tasteful, colorful healthy dish which is ideal to be taken as main meal or as an accompaniment dish. Depending on the filling, the smoky flavor enriches the taste of the stuffed vegetables and become tasty.

Ingredients:

- ➢ 4 large bell peppers, tops cut off and seeds removed
- ➢ 1 cup cooked quinoa or rice
- ➢ 1 can black beans, drained and rinsed
- ➢ 1 cup corn kernels

- ➢ 1 cup diced tomatoes
- ➢ 1 cup shredded cheese (optional)
- ➢ 1 tablespoon olive oil
- ➢ 2 cloves garlic, minced
- ➢ 1 teaspoon cumin
- ➢ 1 teaspoon chili powder
- ➢ Salt and pepper to taste
- ➢ Fresh cilantro, chopped, for garnish

Instructions:

- Prepare the Grill with smokiness suitable for the type of food that you are intending to cook and for the current Traeger Grill temperature settings, set the grill to 350°F.

- In a large bowl, mix, cooked quinoa or rice, black-beans, corn, diced tomatoes, olive oil, minced garlic, cumin powder, chili powder, salt, and pepper. Mix well.

- Place the bell peppers, with the hollowed outside facing up, and fill the cavity with the quinoa mixture, being very careful to make sure the cavity is packed tightly.

- In this arrangement, it is recommended that the stuffed peppers be placed directly on the grill grates.

- 6 BBQ for about an hour until the peppers are soft and the filling is hot.

- Take off from the grill and then plate the food on a serving basin.

- For some additional color and taste, garnish with chopped fresh cilantro; then serve immediately. Taste the delicious smoky stuffed peppers at home without ever leaving your kitchen.

Tips:

- o In case of getting a cheesy variant, one can place shredded cheese over the peppers at the final five to ten mins of the smoking process.

- o Pair it up with salsa alongside avocado slices and it can indeed constitute a meal on its own.

- o It is better if you prepare the stuffing a day before then keep in the refrigerator until needed.

8.3 Grilled Vegetable Skewers

Serves: 6

Cooking Time: 15 minutes

Temperature: 400°F

Grilled vegetable skewer dishes are not only beautiful and interesting but also very useful, when included in the dish. They do not take a long time to prepare and cook and can be suitable for a backyard event or a simple dinner at home.

Ingredients:

- ➤ 2 zucchinis, sliced into rounds
- ➤ 2 bell peppers, cut into chunks
- ➤ 1 red onion, cut into chunks
- ➤ 1 pint cherry tomatoes
- ➤ 2 tablespoons olive oil
- ➤ 2 cloves garlic, minced
- ➤ Salt and pepper to taste
- ➤ Fresh basil, chopped, for garnish

Instructions:

- First, set your Traeger Grill to 400°F before you attempt to cook the dish.

- Cut the zucchini, bell peppers, red onion and cherry tomatoes into portions and place on skewers.

- Next, preparing the marinade that will give a nice flavor to the chicken, combine the olive oil, minced garlic, salt, and pepper in a small bowl.

- Drizzle the olive oil over the vegetable skewers to grease them and apply the spices and herbs on the oil.

- You can stand the skewers upright on the grill racks directly.

- Griddle for about 15 minutes, on flipping in between such that the vegetables soften while having a browned surface.

- Carefully transfer it to a servant platter once you finish grilling the fish.

- Serve with Chopped fresh basil garnishing and enjoy it immediately. These grilled vegetable skewers have the smoky and juicy taste that is hard to find in oven-cooked dishes.

Tips:

○ When barbecuing any food, especially foods that do not come off the grill easily, consider using wooden skewers, however, these should be soaked in water for at least 30 minutes to avoid them catching fire.

○ It can be served with a side of hummus or tzatziki sauce for dipping the pieces in.

○ For these skewers, you can use any of your preferred vegetables just ensure that you mix them as per your desired combination.

8.4 Smoked Cauliflower Steaks

Serves: 4

Cooking Time: 45 minutes

Temperature: 350°F

Smoked cauliflower steaks are a great product which can be preferable to meat; it is low-calorie and very useful. The concept of smoking helps to give the cauliflower a unique, powerful taste that can make it a truly inviting dish.

Ingredients:

➢ 1 large head of cauliflower
➢ 3 tablespoons olive oil
➢ 2 cloves garlic, minced
➢ 1 teaspoon smoked paprika
➢ 1 teaspoon cumin
➢ Salt and pepper to taste

> ➤ Fresh parsley, chopped, for garnish

Instructions:

- First, prepare the Traeger Grill for cooking by turning on your grill and bringing temperature of it to 350 degrees.

- Cut off the darkest green leaves from the cauliflower and trim the damaged or brown section of the main stem. Cut up the head of the cauliflower into thick steaks, every one inch thick.

- In a small bowl, I combined 2 tablespoons of olive oil, 2 cloves of minced garlic, ½ teaspoon of smoked paprika, ½ teaspoon of cumin, a pinch of salt and pepper.

- Coat each of the cauliflower steaks on both sides and then drizzle some olive oil mixture over them.

- This should now be placed right on the direct grilling platform with the steaks.

- Bake for about 45 to 1 hour, the cauliflower should be tender and an attractive dark brown on the surface when fully grilled.

- Take out the cupcakes from the grill and place it in a chafing dish.

- For garnishing, garnish with chopped fresh parsley and then serve the scones immediately. Taste the smokiness, backed with spices, from the delights of smoked cauliflower steaks.

Tips:

- o it is best eaten with some chimichurri sauce or a tahini dressing to increase on its taste.

- o To spice it up a notch, you can yourself some crushed red pepper or even cayenne pepper to the olive oil.

- o In case the cauliflower steaks begin to break down while cooking, the utilization of a grill mat may prevent this from happening.

8.5 Grilled Corn on the Cob

Serves: 6

Cooking Time: 20 minutes

Temperature: 375°F

Cooking corn on the grill can also be quite a delight especially during the summer when the corn has come of age, hence full of taste. The dish is simple to make and is a hot favorite among people cooking outdoors like at barbecues and picnics.

Ingredients:

- ➢ 6 ears of corn, husks removed
- ➢ 3 tablespoons butter, melted
- ➢ 1 teaspoon paprika
- ➢ Salt and pepper to taste
- ➢ Fresh cilantro, chopped, for garnish
- ➢ Lime wedges for serving

Instructions:

- Set your Traeger Grill to high heat to smoke at about 375°F.

- Use a brush to coat the outer surface of the ears of corn in melted butter, and then dust the paprika, salt, and pepper over them.

- Grill the corn with the silks side up to avoid the silks getting burnt or sticking on the grill bottom.

- Grill them for 20 to 25 minutes and turn from time to time until the corn has become tender and a bit caramelized.

- After cooking, transfer and serve it on a serving dish or a large platter.

- Serve hot and garnish with chopped fresh coriander leaves and you can accompany with wedges of lime. Savor corn cooked with smokey barbeque feel to it with this grilled corn on the cob.

Tips:

- o To add an added zest, paint the corn with a concoction of melted butter and crushed garlic before barbecuing.

- o Recommended to have it accompanied with a little sprinkle of Parmesan cheese and a pinch of chili powder to make it more Mexican style.

- o You can also decide to grill the corn with the husks still intact or boil them and when grilling remove the husk, soak the corn in water for 30 minutes.

8.6 Smoked Eggplant Parmesan

Serves: 4

Cooking Time: 1. 5 hours

Temperature: 350°F

Grilled eggplant Parmesan with smoked flavor is a healthy, mouthwatering tasty vegetarian dish which goes well in every table, for a simple lunch or dinner it is a perfect dish to serve.

Ingredients:

- ➢ 2 large eggplants, sliced into rounds
- ➢ 2 cups marinara sauce
- ➢ 2 cups shredded mozzarella cheese
- ➢ 1 cup grated Parmesan cheese
- ➢ 1 cup breadcrumbs
- ➢ 2 tablespoons olive oil
- ➢ 2 cloves garlic, minced
- ➢ Salt and pepper to taste
- ➢ Fresh basil, chopped, for garnish

Instructions:

- So, to start this recipe, fire up your Traeger Grill to 350 degrees F.

- Prepare the eggplant by washing and cutting into one-quarter inch-thick slices for grilling, brush with olive oil and sprinkle with garlic, salt, and pepper.

- Grill the eggplant slices right on the grates of the grill for about 45 minutes or so, or until they are good and soft, getting even a little burnt.

- Take it back to a cooler part of the grill and lower the heat to about 110°C.

- To begin with, the process of using the guidelines, take a little marinara sauce and put it on the bottom of a baking dish. Next, you should put the smoked eggplant slices in layers on top.

- Then spread crumb, mozzarella cheese, and grated parmesan cheese on top.

- Layer again and again till every ingredient has been utilized, and the last layer put on is cheese.

- Place the baking dish back onto the grill and bake for another 45 minutes until the cheese is melted with a gooey surface.

- Take it out of the grill and let it stay a little longer dormant and ready for the consumers' embrace for about 10 minutes.

- Serve accompanied with freshly chopped basil and then set to be served immediately. Take the taste of your average eggplant Parmesan up a notch by using the smoke method to add an extra layer of flavor.

Tips:

- To accompany this dish, you can prepare a garlic bread or side salad of lettuce for that complete meal experience.

- For a slightly spicier sauce, one can add a tiny amount of red pepper flakes to the marinara sauce.

- For those of you who do not know, you can set aside the portions that you did not fully consume to be placed in the fridge which can then be reheated the following day and served immediately.

8.7 Grilled asparagus with lemon zest

Serves: 4

Cooking Time: 10 minutes

Temperature: 400°F

Lemon grilled asparagus is one of the possible dishes that can be served for breakfast, lunch, or dinner and is easy to prepare. Lemon shines through its brightness in flavor, making the natural sweetness of asparagus even more precious.

Ingredients:

- 1 bunch asparagus, trimmed
- 2 tablespoons olive oil
- Juice of 1 lemon
- Salt and pepper to taste
- Fresh parsley, chopped, for garnish

Instructions:

- Prime your Traeger Grill at a temperature of 400 degrees Fahrenheit.

- Drizzle a little olive oil, then add lemon juice, salt and pepper and mix well before tossing it with the asparagus.

- The next preparation method is as follows: Simply arrange the asparagus onto the grill surface of the grill.

- Grill for about 10 minutes, and rotate the asparagus sticks in between turns with tongs, until asparagus gets a tiny bit charred and gets soft.

- From the grill, take out the food and then placed it on a serving dish.

- Sprinkle some chopped fresh parsley over the top, and it is ready to be enjoyed fresh and immediately. Spice up your food; make grilled asparagus with lemon for a change and enjoy its unique and juicy taste.

Tips:

- It's best when served with a dusting of grated Parmesan cheese on top for deeper flavoring.

- For a splash of difference, the peel of a lemon should be yielded in addition to the juice.

- Grilled asparagus: these can be consumed the following day or used in salads or on pizza toppings.

8.8 Smoked Tomato Soup

Serves: 6

Cooking Time: 1 hour

Temperature: 225°F

This Smoked tomato soup recipe is a delicious, sexy, simple, and warming dish which can serve for almost any season. The process of smoking stirs up a talent of flavors within the tomatoes.

Ingredients:

- ➢ 2 pounds tomatoes, halved
- ➢ 1 large onion, chopped
- ➢ 4 cloves garlic, minced
- ➢ 4 cups vegetable broth
- ➢ 2 tablespoons olive oil
- ➢ Salt and pepper to taste
- ➢ Fresh basil, chopped, for garnish

Instructions:

- To smoke chicken on your Traeger Grill, this is what you should do: As you prepare your chicken ensure that the Traeger Grill temperature is set to 225 degrees.

- Drizzle a little olive oil and season the halved tomatoes with salt and pepper.

- Lay the tomatoes cut side down directly on the grill grates without using even a single piece of foil wrap.

- After 30 minutes, stir the tomatoes and cook for another 30 additional minutes or until tomatoes are soften and slightly caramelized.

- Take it from the grill and move it to a large pot Add to this pot the following **Ingredients:**

- Sauté the onion and chop it, mince the garlic, and put the vegetable broth.

- Boil and then unresolved, cook for at least 20 minutes.

- Bring the soup mixture to the serving temperature and then blend the soup until getting the smooth consistency using an immersion blender.

- Season with additional salt and pepper to taste.

- There is nothing as perfect as giving the recipe a final touch by adjusting the needed quantity of the amount of salt and pepper that is required in the preparation of the recipe.

- Sprinkle with finely chopped fresh basil before you serve the rice dish freshly. Indulge in the smoky taste of tomato soup that are prepared through smoking.

Tips:

- Grill some cheese sandwich and serve with this as a perfect match…

- As a special touch for a richer taste, pour a teaspoon of balsamic vinegar when the soup is almost done and only the soup has to be blended.

- Any leftover soup should be left in an airtight container in the refrigerator so that it can be heated every time it is needed to make a quick dish.

8.9 Grilled Brussels Sprouts

Serves: 4

Cooking Time: 25 minutes

Temperature: 375°F

The recipe of grilled Brussels sprouts is simple yet delicious and nutritious that can be a perfect side dish. These fruits benefit from grilling cooking since it enhances the natural sweetness of the fruit while giving it a smoky taste.

Ingredients:

- 1 pound Brussels sprouts, trimmed and halved
- 2 tablespoons olive oil
- 2 cloves garlic, minced
- Salt and pepper to taste
- Fresh lemon juice for serving

Instructions:

- It is good to prepare your Traeger Grill for cooking for at least fifteen minutes at 375°F.

- First prepare and season the Brussels sprouts by drizzling with olive oil, garlic, and salt and pepper to taste.

- To grill brussels sprouts, arrange the vegetables directly on the grill grate or, better yet, in a grill wok.

- Grill for approximately 25 minutes but flip occasionally to ensure that the minimum of the Brussels sprouts is concurrently browning, with the tops becoming slightly charred.

- These may then be pulled out from the grill and served on a platter.

- After that add some amount of lemon juice and mix it well then serve immediately. Try succulent Brussels sprouts cooked on a grill: the crisp flavors of smoke infuse the vegetable with extra sweetness.

Tips:

- Garnish with a little grated Parmesan cheese to enhance the taste. It can be served with a garnished sprinkle of little grated Parmesan cheese.

- To add some heat, grill this pizza with red pepper flakes giving it a spicy touch.

- The cooked Brussels sprouts can be served in salads or cooked with a little bit of oil and garlic and served as a side dish to roasted meats.

- 8. The cheese sauce is prepared by combining butter, flour, milk, onion, dry mustard, salt, and pepper: In large casserole, layer half each of the milk and macaroni; sprinkle with cheese bread crumbs, and dot with butter In medium bowl, mix butter food; stir in flour, salt, pepper, mustard and milk Cook over low heat until butter melts Place macaroni in greased 2 quart ovenproof c

8.10 Smoked Mac and Cheese

Serves: 8

Cooking Time: 1. 5 hours

Temperature: 225°F

Cheesy macaroni dish is a dish that is very splendid and delicious to be served anytime. The smoky flavor of the bacon not only contribute to that kind of unique taste into that classic comfort food.

Ingredients:

- ➢ 1 pound elbow macaroni
- ➢ 4 cups shredded cheddar cheese
- ➢ 2 cups shredded mozzarella cheese
- ➢ 2 cups milk
- ➢ 1 cup heavy cream
- ➢ 1/2 cup butter
- ➢ 1/2 cup all-purpose flour
- ➢ 1 tablespoon Dijon mustard
- ➢ Salt and pepper to taste
- ➢ 1 cup breadcrumbs
- ➢ 2 tablespoons melted butter
- ➢ Fresh parsley, chopped, for garnish

Instructions:

- Always set your Traeger Grill to the lowest temperature of 225 degrees Fahrenheit before you start grilling.

- The elbow macaroni should be cooked in boiling water accordingly to package instructions but should remain firm. Drain and set aside.

- In a large pot, melt the butter over medium heat – Add the butter and let it melt over medium heat, stirring occasionally. Sauté the flour and cook the mixture for 1-2 mins until a light brown.

- SLOWLY stir in the milk and heavy cream, stirring continuously until the sauce is thickened.

- Withdraw from the heat and add the shredded cheddar cheese, shredded mozzarella cheese, and Dijon mustard to the mix and stir the mix until the cheese has melted, and the sauce has thinned.

- Add little salt and black pepper to your desire.

- Add this to cooked macaroni and stir till well incorporated.

- Place the mac and cheese into an oven safe dish for the next step.

- Trust me, put your breadcrumbs with melted butter on the side of mac and cheese and serve.

- Ensure that the baking dish is positioned on the grill grates without being enclosed in any foil or aluminum paper.

- Smoke for about 1. 5 hours more, or until the top has turned golden brown and the macaroni and cheese are thoroughly melted.

- Transfer it to a plate and let the chicken stand on the grill for at least 10 minutes while you organize the rest of the food or prepare the sides.

- There's no need for any fancy presentation – garnish with fresh chopped parsley and serve immediately. Indulge in the savory, cheesy goodness of our smoked macaroni and cheese dishes.

Tips:

- For an added twist, feel free to combine a couple of the cheeses such as Gruyere, fontina, or smoked gouda.

- You can use bacon that is cooked and added to the mac and cheese or can have cooked smoked sausage as a variation on this recipe.

- For instance, if they do not finish eating mac and cheese during the first sitting it can be either baked or microwaved the next time.

Chapter 9: Desserts on the Grill

Yes, you read that right—desserts on the grill! This chapter is all about satisfying your sweet tooth with a smoky twist. Grilling and smoking desserts add a unique flavor profile that elevates your favorite treats to new heights.
Imagine biting into a warm, gooey grilled chocolate chip cookie or enjoying the caramelized sweetness of grilled bananas in a banana split. From smoked apple crisp to grilled s'mores, these recipes will make your grill the star of dessert time.

We've included a variety of options, from classic favorites like peach cobbler and brownies to more adventurous treats like grilled pears with honey. Each recipe is designed to bring out the best in your desserts, adding a smoky, grilled flavor that's sure to impress. So, let's end our meals on a high note and make dessert time an unforgettable experience.

9.1 Grilled Chocolate Chip Cookies

Serves: 8

Cooking Time: 15 minutes

Temperature: 375°F

Grilled marshmallows are a nice touch when placed in original chocolate chip cookies. It is important to cook the chocolate for the right amount of time to melt it as the grill adds a slight hint of smoke to the cookies.

Ingredients:

- 1 cup butter, softened
- 1 cup granulated sugar
- 1 cup brown sugar, packed
- 2 large eggs
- 1 teaspoon vanilla extract
- 3 cups all-purpose flour
- 1 teaspoon baking soda
- 1/2 teaspoon salt
- 2 cups chocolate chips

Instructions:

- If using the kit with a and Traeger Grill, then the grilling temperature should be set to 375 degrees F.

- To the bowl of a stand mixer or a large mixing bowl, add the butter, granulated sugar, and brown sugar and mix on high until smooth and fluffy.

- Add the eggs, one at a time, and beat on low speed before adding the vanilla extract and mixing well.

- In a measuring cup combine the flour, baking soda and salt together by shaking the ingredients in the cup.

- Slowly fold the dry ingredients with the wet mixture and only combine the ingredients until they are not fully incorporated.

- Pour the chocolate chips and fold them into the batter.

- Place small round tablespoons of the dough on greased cookie sheet.

- A baking sheet should be placed directly on the surface of the grill.
- Therefore, a baking sheet should be directly placed on the grill grates.

- As for cooking, grill for about 15 minutes, or until edges of the cakes are cooked caramel-like golden brown and the centers are firm.

- Alight the grill and let the chops cool on a wire rack before serving. Feel the sandwich cookies' warmth, thickness, and hint of smoke.

Tips:

o For an added incentive to enhance the taste of the cookies, dip a little amount of sea salt in the saltshaker and then spread it on the cookies before grilling them.

o It is recommended that these cookies are best served while they're still hot with a side of vanilla ice cream.

o Freezing is another way of preserving the dish Provided with any leftover food, you should put it in an air-tight container so that it can stay fresh.

9.2 Smoked Apple Crisp

Serves: 6

Cooking Time: 1 hour

Temperature: 350°F

Apple crisp is easy and satisfying dessert most of all it has sweet and sour taste of apples, with butter graham cracker crumb topping. When you add smoke into the recipe, the food feels special and has a different and special taste.

Ingredients:

- ➢ 6 cups apples, peeled and sliced
- ➢ 1/2 cup granulated sugar
- ➢ 1 teaspoon cinnamon
- ➢ 1/2 teaspoon nutmeg
- ➢ 1 tablespoon lemon juice
- ➢ 1 cup old-fashioned oats
- ➢ 1/2 cup all-purpose flour
- ➢ 1/2 cup brown sugar, packed
- ➢ 1/2 cup butter, melted

Instructions:

- Start with your Traeger Grill and set it to cook at 350°F before you start cooking the dishes.

- In a large bowl take the sliced apple and then add in granulated sugar, cinnamon, nutmeg, and lemon juice and mix it well. Give a quick turn to ensure that the apples are coated with the milk mixture.

- Pour the apple mixture onto a greased baking dish, instead put the apple mixture in a greased baking dish.

- In an Another bowl combine the oats, all-purpose flour, brown sugar & melted butter for the topping – mix until crumbs.

- In simple terms, pour the oats over the apples then spread out the mixture well.

- Put the baking dish on the grill rack top.
- This cooking method is best applied to weber grill models that are equipped with a top rack or a baking pan.

- Bake for about 1 hour, or until the apples are soft and sides of the dish are caramelized, and the top of the dish is crusty.

- And finally, transfer all from the grill and let to cool slightly before serving. Savor the caramelized, smoky notes of apple crisp complemented by a scoop of vanilla ice cream or a spoonful of whipping cream.

Tips:

- ○ When using apples, it is preferred to use more than one type of apples to improve flavor and taste.

- o One can also add a handful of chopped nuts to the topping for that little extra that provides texture.

- o Remainder can be preserved in a refrigerator and these foods can be warmed up in the oven or a microwave.

9.3 Grilled S'mores

Serves: 8

Cooking Time: 5 minutes

Temperature: 400°F

Grilled s'mores are the great dessert recipe that combines one of the most favorite camping delicacies with the taste of a barbecue party. It also adds a hint of smokiness to the topped and tailored softies, which in fact makes them even tastier.

Ingredients:

- ➤ 8 graham crackers, broken in half
- ➤ 8 large marshmallows
- ➤ 8 squares of chocolate

Instructions:

- The recommended temperature setting of your Traeger Grill is 400°F.

- For the crust and topping, line a baking sheet with parchment.

- Place a square of Chocolate on each graham cracker square and another marshmallow.

- Generically speaking, you can place the baking sheet directly on the grates of your grill.

- Grill for about 5 minutes, or until the outer chocolate is gooey and the marshmallows are nicely toasted with streaks of brown on top.

- Carefully transfer the s'mores to a plate, then place the rest of the graham crackers on each layer.

- Consumption should be on the same plate and is great for enjoying the flavor of the s'mores e with the smoky taste of the grill.

Tips:

o To make it even more delicious and interesting, one can use chocolate with different flavors, like dark chocolate, or mint or peanut butter.

o For a little bit of a gourmet type experience, you can put a slice of banana on top or even a dab of peanut butter.

o If you do not have a grill easily accessible, it is also possible to make these s'mores in the oven on the broiler setting.

9.4 Smoked Peach Cobbler

Serves: 6

Cooking Time: 1 hour

Temperature: 350°F

Smoked peach cobbler can be described as a delicious peach dessert containing peaches as well as the dough based on butter. Even letting out a hint of smoke, having a taste is great and gives a touch of an unusual taste.

Ingredients:

- ➤ 6 cups sliced peaches
- ➤ 1/2 cup granulated sugar
- ➤ 1 tablespoon lemon juice
- ➤ 1 teaspoon cinnamon
- ➤ 1 cup all-purpose flour
- ➤ 1 cup granulated sugar
- ➤ 1 tablespoon baking powder
- ➤ 1/2 teaspoon salt
- ➤ 1 cup milk
- ➤ 1/2 cup butter, melted

Instructions:

- Ease your Traeger Grill into the medium heat setting and set the temperature to 350°F.

- Place the sliced peaches into a large bowl, with 1/2 tsp granulated sugar, lemon juice, and cinnamon. Toss to coat the peaches with the sugar and grease evenly.

- Place the peach mixture in a baking dish that has been greased in advance.

- I the other bowl, make sure that you combine the flour, 1 cup granulated sugar, baking powder and salt.

- Add milk and melted butter and through the batter mechanically.

- Spoon the batter over the peaches so that the liquid is evenly spread out over the fruit.

- Indeed, we recommend putting the baking dish simply on the grill grates.

- Allow to braise for about 1 hour or until the top is golden brown or even caramelized and the peaches seem soft.

- After it turns brown on both sides, transfer to a plate and let it rest for some time before serving. Savor the warm, smoky peach cobbler with a scoop that compliments this amazing peach cobbler with vanilla ice cream or gratify your palate with a dollop of whipped cream.

Tips:

- For best results, use fresh and ripe peaches but if fresher peaches are difficult to get then can or frozen peaches are preferred.

- You can also add a pinch of spices such as nutmegs or ginger to the mixture if you want it spicy.

- The preparation that is not consumed immediately can be saved in the refrigerator and then warm it in the oven or in the microwave oven.

9.5 Grilled Banana Splits

Serves: 4

Cooking Time: 10 minutes

Temperature: 375°F

Grilled banana splits are a great variation of the conventional banana splits You can get creative and enjoy this as a delightful dessert. It browns bananas by directly grilling them while intensively sweetening the fruit and adding the smoke shade to it.

Ingredients:

- ➢ 4 bananas, unpeeled
- ➢ 1/4 cup melted butter
- ➢ 1/4 cup brown sugar
- ➢ 1/2 teaspoon cinnamon
- ➢ Ice cream, for serving
- ➢ Chocolate sauce, for drizzling
- ➢ Whipped cream, for topping
- ➢ Maraschino cherries, for garnish

Instructions:

- Bring your Traeger Grill to medium high temperature to around 375 °F before you proceed to cook the chicken.

- Next, in a small bowl prepare the melted butter, brown sugar, and cinnamon mixture.

- Peel each banana and place on a serving plate, then cut each one lengthwise, but not halfway. Peel the bananas and split them horizontally using the knife by making a circle to form a small bowl.

- Spread it on each banana by coating the inside part with the butter mixture you made earlier.

- A great way to prepare the bananas is to put them on the direct heat by placing them directly on the grillery with the cut side facing upwards.

- Cook for around 10 minutes until the banana will be soft and the sugar topping will be caramelized.

- Serve hot and to remove skin from the meat, pull out the whole fillet from the grill and let it rest a few moments before peeling the skin off.

- To serve, place each grilled banana on a bowl and garnish with scoops of the fruity ice cream or gelato, drizzled with chocolate syrup followed by a dollop of whipped cream and a cherry on top. Savor grilled bananas split with a diverse warm and smoky flavor.

Tips:

- If desired, sprinkle with chopped nuts for additional crunchy feeling or spoon a handful of sprinkles for a bit of extra sweet.

- Try using some of the exquisite soft ice cream scents like caramel or peanut butter for a better taste.

- The grilled bananas can also be served as an accompaniment the following day or used in smoothies or as a topping to pancakes or waffles.

9.6 Smoked Brownies

Serves: 8

Cooking Time: 45 minutes

Temperature: 350°F

Smoked brownies are tasty and moist dessert with enhanced chocolate flap with smoky flavor. They will become very popular rather entertaining at any sort of function.

Ingredients:

- 1 cup butter, melted
- 1 cup granulated sugar
- 1 cup brown sugar, packed
- 4 large eggs
- 1 teaspoon vanilla extract
- 1 cup all-purpose flour
- 1 cup cocoa powder
- 1/2 teaspoon salt

> ➢ 1 cup chocolate chips

Instructions:

- First, you should prepare the Traeger Grill with the temperature set at 350°F.

- In the bowl for mixing the wet ingredients, combine the melted butter, granulated sugar, and brown sugar.

- Sieve the flour with salt and baking powder, mix it into the batter and add the eggs, one at a time and finally mix in the vanilla extract.

- In another bowl mix the dry ingredients like flour, cocoa power & salt.

- Gradually, the dry ingredients should be incorporated into the wet ones and until such time that they will just blend a little.

- Melt the chocolates and fold them into the batter gently.

- Pour the batter into a greased baking dish so that we can bake it.

- Put the baking dish straight on the grill while it is on using the grates.

- Bake for about 45 minutes or until when a toothpick inserted in the middle would come out slightly sticky.

- Transfer the cookies to a cooling rack, allowing them to cool completely before using a knife to slice them into squares. Savor the tasty, moist, and flavorful smoky brownies that takes your palate on a tour of textures and flavors.

Tips:

- To elevate the luxury levels even further, serve warm brownies with a scoop of ice cream and a dose of caramel sauce.

- It's best to add nuts or dried fruit into the batter and this will enhance the resultant cake.

- To keep the Leftovers fresh and to avoid compromising their nutrients, they should be stored in an airtight container.

9.7 Grilled Pears with Honey

Serves: 4

Cooking Time: 15 minutes

Temperature: 375°F

This recipe of Grilled pears with honey is a very basic and yet very refined one which allows the natural flavor of the pears be highlighted. This caramelizes the pears, also adding some griddle smokiness that works well with the honey.

Ingredients:

> ➢ 4 pears, halved and cored
> ➢ 2 tablespoons melted butter
> ➢ 1/4 cup honey
> ➢ 1 teaspoon cinnamon
> ➢ Vanilla ice cream, for serving

Instructions:

- Turn your Traeger Grill control knob to 375°F.

- Melt butter, then pat the cut parts of the pears with the butter.

- Slice the pears in less than half and face them downwards on the grills.

- It takes approximately 10 minutes to grill the pears depending on how tender you want them to be and those attractive grill lines.

- Cut the pears lengthwise into quarters, open them up and place them in the honey mixture, brushing it well and set them on the baking tray with the honey-side up, top it with ground cinnamon.

- Grill for an additional 5 minutes, or until the honey browning up on the steaks.

- It is best served hot; thus, once you turn them over on the grill, transfer the grilled bananas to a plate and serve it hot topped with a scoop of vanilla ice cream. Grilled pears with honey: capturing the essence of barbeque competition with a sweet and slightly charred taste.

Tips:

- It is recommended to use overripe but still hard pears as such pears will be perfect in terms of texture and taste.

- Toss a spoonful of chopped nuts for additional texture.

- Conversely, any leftover grilled pears may be utilized in a salad, as a garnish for oatmeal, or in yogurt.

9.8 Smoked Bread Pudding

Serves: 6

Cooking Time: 1 hour

Temperature: 325°F

Smoked bread pudding is a luxury dessert of the cravings that are easily satisfied with a touch of smoking. The smoke envelops the bread and infusing it into this scrumptious and traditional sweet which is Tiramisu.

Ingredients:

- 6 cups cubed day-old bread
- 2 cups milk
- 1 cup heavy cream
- 3/4 cup granulated sugar
- 3 large eggs
- 1 teaspoon vanilla extract
- 1/2 teaspoon cinnamon
- 1/4 teaspoon nutmeg
- 1/2 cup raisins or chocolate chips (optional)
- Caramel sauce, for serving

Instructions:

- First preheat the grill of your Traeger at 325: °F.

- Combine the milk, heavy cream, sugar, eggs, Vanillas, Cinnamon, and Nutmeg in a large bowl.

- Finally toss in the cubed bread, ensuring that its fully well coated. Allow it to steep for another fifteen minutes to help it soak the liquid up.

- Add the raisins/chocolate chips in case you were using them.

- Pour this mixture into a greased baking dish.

- Lastly, replace the baking dish over the grill grates especially if you intend to finish cooking the meal through grilling.

- Let the skillet cook for about an hour, or until the top layer becomes a beautiful golden-brown color and the center is firm.

- This done, remove the shrimps from the grill and let them cool for a few minutes before serving.

- You can pour some caramel sauce over it and serve it warm. Indulge in smoked bread pudding, now served on dining tables with a delightful taste of smoke in every bite.

Tips:

- For example, other types of bread could be used, like challah or brioche for a chewier, more complex texture.

- Incorporate bourbon or rum into the custard mixture as a way of enhancing the flavor of the food.

- The remnants can be kept in the refrigerator to be warmed in an oven or microwave oven all the same.

9.9 Grilled Cinnamon Apples

Serves: 4

Cooking Time: 20 minutes

Temperature: 375°F

One of the many healthy and delicious treats out there, grilled cinnamon apples are an excellent desert for any occasion. This forms a nice caramel layer to the apples as they get cooked while also giving them a smoky flavor.

Ingredients:

> - 4 apples, halved and cored
> - 2 tablespoons melted butter
> - 1/4 cup brown sugar
> - 1 teaspoon cinnamon
> - Vanilla ice cream, for serving

Instructions:

- The recommended heat level to prepare this dish on your Traeger Grill is at 375 °F.

- That is, use a pastry brush to baste the cut sides of cut apples with melted butter.

- Take another bowl and to it add the brown sugar and cinnamon together.

- In a separate bowl, I mixed White sugar and brown sugar, then pour this on the cut sides of the apples.

- Grilling Apples: As with the peaches, put the apples face down directly on the grill surfaces.

- About 15 minutes of grilling should suffice depending on the grill marks or until the apples become tender.

- The sugar mixture has to be caramelized so turn the apples and grill for 5 minutes more in total.

- Once done, remove from the grill and share immediately while still hot with a scoop of vanilla ice cream. Treat yourself to this scrumptious and smoky take on the season's best ingredient: grilled cinnamon apples!

Tips:

- Make sure you don't use mushy apples for this recipe; it's recommended to use Granny Smith or Honey crisp apples.

- For toppings try a sprinkling of chopped nuts or granola to add an extra crunchy texture.

- The grilled apples, which are left after the filming, it is possible to add them to oatmeal or use as topping to pancakes and waffles.

9.10 Smoked Lemon Bars

Serves: 8

Cooking Time: 1 hour

Temperature: 325°F

Smoked lemon bars are delicious and sweet and have a flavor that is unique to the smoked food preparation method. The lemon filling is yummy when combined with the buttery-sweet pastry and the sugar-water-zest makes the mouth-watering lemon color richer.

Ingredients:

- 1 cup all-purpose flour
- 1/2 cup powdered sugar
- 1/2 cup butter, melted
- 4 large eggs
- 1 1/2 cups granulated sugar
- 1/4 cup all-purpose flour
- 1/2 teaspoon baking powder
- 1/2 cup lemon juice
- Powdered sugar, for dusting

Instructions:

- In this case, set your Traeger grills to approximately 163°C.

- Whisk 1 cup flour and 1/2 cup powdered sugar in a medium bowl using a whisk.

- Mix in the melted butter till the contents of the mixture are evenly blended.

- Pat the mixture into the bottom and sides of a greased tin.

- Finally place the baking dish on the grill grates of the barbecue without the use of the lid.

- Bake for about 20 minutes, or until it is adequately browned on top and golden brown on the bottom.

- In a separate bowl, mix eggs as well as granulated sugar, 1/4 cup flour, and baking powder and lemon juice.

- After baking these crusts, pour over this lemon mixture.

- Bake it for about half an hour, 30-35 minutes, or until you notice that the filling is no longer moveable in the cake mixture and the top is just slightly browned.

- Transfer to a serving plate, allow to cool for a few minutes and then chill into the refrigerator.

- Dust surface of the cake with powdered sugar before slicing to serve as squares. Savor the pleasure of juicy lemon bars smoked to perfection.

Tips:

o You can also make fresh lemon juice for enhanced flavor of the dish.

o This makes it extremely important to incorporate a zest from a lemon to the filling to enhance the brightness.

o A leftover lemon bar, sweet or savory, can be stored inside the fridge and eaten cold or warmed to room temperature.

Chapter 10: Sauces, Rubs, and Marinades

No great grill expert is complete without a repertoire of incredible sauces, rubs, and marinades. This chapter is your secret weapon for adding layers of flavor to your grilled and smoked dishes. Whether you're looking for a classic BBQ sauce, a spicy dry rub, or a tangy marinade, we've got you covered.

Discover the bold flavors of smoky chipotle sauce, the sweet and tangy perfection of honey mustard glaze, and the robust taste of Mediterranean herb marinade. Each recipe is designed to complement your grilled and smoked creations, enhancing their natural flavors, and adding a delicious twist.

These sauces, rubs, and marinades are easy to make and versatile, perfect for experimenting and finding your signature flavor. Let's dive into the world of flavor boosters and take your grilling to the next level.

10.1 Classic BBQ Sauce

Worcestershire-based BBQ sauce is a tasty and all-purpose sauce ideal for marinating and basting meat and fish before grilling and smoking. But it has been well sweetened and yet tangy and smoky to become the sauce that is perfect for rubbing on, ribs, chicken, and others.

Ingredients:

- 2 cups ketchup
- 1/2 cup apple cider vinegar
- 1/4 cup brown sugar
- 1/4 cup molasses
- 1 tablespoon Worcestershire sauce
- 1 tablespoon smoked paprika
- 1 teaspoon garlic powder
- 1 teaspoon onion powder
- 1/2 teaspoon black pepper
- 1/2 teaspoon salt
- 1/4 teaspoon cayenne pepper (optional)

Instructions:

- Stir together all the ingredients in a saucepan that can comfortably accommodate the mixture.

- Florets to boil, for medium heat 8-10 minutes, stirring from time to time.

- Bring to a boil over medium heat then reduce heat to low and continue to cook the sauce for 20 more minutes stirring often.

- Stir well and when it is hot enough, transfer from the heat source, then allow it to cool. Take treats within 2 or 3 hours or store the residue covered in a refrigerator for up to 2 weeks.

Tips:

- o Increase the heat by adding more cayenne pepper or increase the sweet element with more brown sugar.

- o This sauce is versatile, use it to make a base and modify it with whatever fixings you desire, some choices include adding a little bourbon or liquid smoke.

10.2 Spicy Dry Rub

This is ideal for you to use as a dry rub to add spice to the grilled or the smoked meats that you are preparing. Browning mixture of spices to develop a crust that makes positively enrich the taste of meat, particularly the beef, pork, and chicken.

Ingredients:

- ➢ 2 tablespoons brown sugar
- ➢ 1 tablespoon smoked paprika
- ➢ 1 tablespoon chili powder
- ➢ 1 tablespoon black pepper
- ➢ 1 tablespoon garlic powder
- ➢ 1 tablespoon onion powder
- ➢ 1 teaspoon cayenne pepper
- ➢ 1 teaspoon ground cumin
- ➢ 1 teaspoon salt

Instructions:

- To make the rub, put the following ingredients in a small bowl: brown sugar, salt, paprika, garlic powder, onion powder, and black pepper.

- That is all you are expected to do with the paste; apply it liberally all over your preferred meat type.

- When grilling or smoking the meat one has to make sure that it should be allowed to stand for at least 30 minutes to lose its shape and to allow the flavor to be assimilated.

Tips:

- o This is best done by transferring any remaining rub into an airtight container that should be stored at room temperature in a cool dry place for up to three months.

- o Despite its particularity, this rub can also be enjoyable on vegetables or tofu if the preparation of a spicy dish is desired.

10.3 Mediterranean Herb Marinade

This Mediterranean Herb Marinade is easy to make and made combining fresh herbs, garlic and lemon juice and is great used on for chicken, lamb, or fish. It adds a beautiful, bright flavor and aroma to all your dishes that is hard to achieve with regular pepper.

Ingredients:

- ➢ 1/4 cup olive oil
- ➢ 1/4 cup lemon juice
- ➢ 3 cloves garlic, minced
- ➢ 2 tablespoons fresh oregano, chopped
- ➢ 2 tablespoons fresh rosemary, chopped
- ➢ 2 tablespoons fresh thyme, chopped
- ➢ 1 teaspoon salt
- ➢ 1/2 teaspoon black pepper

Instructions:

- In a bowl, whisk together the olive oil, lemon juice, garlic, oregano, rosemary, thyme, salt, and pepper.

- A popular method is to put your meat or fish in a re-sealable plastic bag then pour the marinade over the meat/fish.

- Tie the end of the bag and marinate it, preferably in the refrigerator for 2 hours to overnight for better tastes.

- Take off the marinade and cook it over the grill or through smoking according to a particular method.

Tips:

- In the same manner, it is best to use vegetables that you want to be softer to be marinated in this. It is nice served with zucchinis, bell peppers or mushrooms.

- It requires that for a more enhanced taste of the herbs and garlic, one should double the quantities indicated above.

10.4 Garlic Herb Butter

Garlic herb butter is yet another mouth-watering seasoning that can be applied to dishes such as grilled meat, vegetables, or bread. One more thing that all kinds of olives have in common is their taste… or better said – their richness: It is very rich in flavor, making any dish luxurious.

Ingredients:

- 1/2 cup unsalted butter, softened
- 3 cloves garlic, minced
- 2 tablespoons fresh parsley, chopped
- 1 tablespoon fresh thyme, chopped
- 1 teaspoon lemon zest
- 1/2 teaspoon salt
- 1/4 teaspoon black pepper

Instructions:

- In a smaller bowl mix the butter, garlic, parsley, thyme, lemon rind, salt, and pepper with a spoon until combined.

- Stir them well till all the ingredients combine well, forming a smooth batter.

- After doing so, pick up the butter and transfer it onto a piece of plastic wrap before shaping it into a log form.

- Keep refrigerated; it is recommended that it should be served after it has been refrigerated for at least an hour.

Tips:

- o This butter can be placed in the refrigerator for up to 14 days or freezer for up to 90 days.

- o This butter can be used as a final table butter basting grilled steaks, fish or corn on the cob are delicious.

10.5 Honey Mustard Glaze

Honey mustard glaze is a sweet and sour sauce that can be used for basting chickens that have been grilled or barbequed or for any other potassium rich food like pork, salmon and so on. What is most appealing about it is that the honey caramelizes most nicely on the grill, leaving a sticky layer.

Ingredients:

- ➢ 1/2 cup honey
- ➢ 1/4 cup Dijon mustard
- ➢ 2 tablespoons apple cider vinegar
- ➢ 1 tablespoon soy sauce
- ➢ 1 teaspoon garlic powder
- ➢ 1/2 teaspoon black pepper

Instructions:

- To make the marinade, in a medium bowl, combine honey, Dijon, apple cider vinegar, soy sauce, garlic powder, black pepper and whisk vigorously.

- Apply the glaze towards the last 10 minutes of grilling or smoking, painting it with a brush on your meat.

- Put any more glazes left into a dish and use as a dip for the overs.

Tips:

- o This glaze can be made a day or so ahead and refrigerated, up to one week in advance.

- o Taste the batter and add more honey if it needs more sweetness or reduce on it if the batter has too much sweetness.

10.6 Asian Teriyaki Marinade

Asian teriyaki marinade refers to a compound that is prepared from soy sauce, ginger, and garlic which is ideal for use with beef, chicken, or vegetables. It is instrumental in giving the most desired and rich taste to your meals- the umami.

Ingredients:

- 1/2 cup soy sauce
- 1/4 cup brown sugar
- 1/4 cup rice vinegar
- 2 tablespoons sesame oil
- 3 cloves garlic, minced
- 1 tablespoon fresh ginger, grated
- 1 teaspoon red pepper flakes (optional)
- 1/4 cup water

Instructions:

- Soak the chicken pieces in the marinade made by combining the soy sauce, brown sugar, rice vinegar, sesame oil, minced garlic, minced ginger, red pepper flakes (optional), and water until the brown sugar dissolves.

- Prepare your meat or vegetables and put them in a zip lock back before pouring the marinade over the contents of the bag.

- Then, close the bag and keep it in the refrigerator for at least an hour, to unfathomable preference overnight.

- Take it from marinade and cook on direct heat by grilling or smoking for the desired result.

Tips:

- This marinade is long and rich, especially suitable for tofu or mushrooms if you wanted a vegetarian dish.

- Use a portion of it to mix with meat to pour over the remaining portion of marinade to be used as sauce.

10.7 Smoky Chipotle Sauce

It may be spicy and smoky with a nice char to it – you can use it to enhance those grilled or smoked foods. It is versatile at it can be used as a dip, or as a topping for foods like burgers and tacos.

Ingredients:

- ➤ 1 cup mayonnaise
- ➤ 2 chipotle peppers in adobo sauce, minced
- ➤ 1 tablespoon adobo sauce (from the can of chipotle peppers)
- ➤ 1 tablespoon lime juice
- ➤ 1 teaspoon garlic powder
- ➤ 1/2 teaspoon smoked paprika
- ➤ Salt and pepper to taste

Instructions:

- Prepare Chipotle Spread by combining in a bowl: mayonnaise, minced chipotle peppers, adobo sauce, lime juice, garlic powder, smoked paprika and stirring until smooth.

- Season the mixture with salt & pepper to suite your taste.

- Chill the dish for at least half an hour before consuming to enable the flavors to improve, which are usually locked in by cold temperatures.

Tips:

- o Please use an extension cord that is at least 50 feet long when grilling tacos on a charcoal grill.

- o This sauce should be placed covered in the refrigerator it can be stored for up to one week.

10.8 Lemon Pepper Rub

Lemon pepper rub is a tasty blend excellent for use in preparing BBQ chicken, fish and many more vegetables. This variety has a bright lemon tang to it and cracked black pepper and integrates itself quickly into your flavor palette.

Ingredients:

- 2 tablespoons lemon zest
- 1 tablespoon cracked black pepper
- 1 tablespoon sea salt
- 1 teaspoon garlic powder
- 1 teaspoon onion powder
- 1 teaspoon dried thyme

Instructions:

- First, put the lemon zest, cracked black pepper, sea salt, garlic powder, onion powder, and dried thyme together in a bowl of yours.

- Stiff peak – Beat the egg whites until stiff peaks form.

- Aside from that, it is advisable to apply the mixture richly on your meat or vegetables before BBQing or smoking them.

Tips:

- This rub is excellent on grilled asparagus or roasted potatoes.

- To enhance the flavor of the lemon even further, just before removing the pan from heat or after plating, squeeze in a little lemon juice.

10.9 Maple Bourbon Glaze

Maple bourbon glaze is a delectable and glossy sauce, a sticky and sweet entrée for pork, chicken, or salmon. Maple syrup with bourbon makes for a twisted sticky and tasty glaze that coats the poultry well.

Ingredients:

- 1/2 cup maple syrup
- 1/4 cup bourbon
- 2 tablespoons Dijon mustard
- 1 tablespoon soy sauce
- 1 teaspoon garlic powder

> ➤ 1/2 teaspoon black pepper

Instructions:

- In a small saucepan, mix the maple syrup, bourbon, Dijon mustard, soy sauce, garlic powder, black pepper.

- Allow it to heat until it boils gently, stirring frequently at the same time.

- Turn the heat down to low and allow the glaze to cook for about 10-15 minutes, resisting the urge to let it reach the rolling boil stage as it will be too thick.

- Stir and then leave to cool the above instructions are normally written under the special use of a vessel in the cooking process. Any leftover should be consumed on the spot or be placed in an airtight container and stored in the refrigerator for up to 7 days.

Tips:

- ○ Apply the glaze during the final ten minutes of grilling or smoking to avoid burning the glaze onto the exterior surface of the meat.

- ○ If you want to avoid using and alcohol, replace the bourbon with apple cider for a delicious taste.

10.10 Cajun Spice Mix

Cajun spice mix is a blend of spices which is quite hot and aromatic to add flavor to the grills and smoked foods. this one is perfect on chicken, shrimp, n other vegetables.

Ingredients:

- ➤ 2 tablespoons paprika
- ➤ 1 tablespoon garlic powder
- ➤ 1 tablespoon onion powder
- ➤ 1 tablespoon dried oregano
- ➤ 1 tablespoon dried thyme
- ➤ 1 tablespoon black pepper
- ➤ 1 tablespoon white pepper

> ➤ 1 teaspoon cayenne pepper
> ➤ 1 teaspoon salt

Instructions:

- In a bowl, place the following Ingredients: the paprika, garlic powder, onion powder, dried oregano, dried thyme, black pepper, white pepper, cayenne pepper, and salt, and blend until evenly mixed.

- Among the best practices for handling the spice mix is to store it in an airtight jar.

- When preparing to barbecue this, make sure you apply the mixture to your meat or vegetables before grilling or smoking.

Tips:

- These can be adjusted based on preferences and the amount of heat which can be increased or decreased by the amount of cayenne peppers used.

- That's why it's equally useful for marinating fries or putting on roasted nuts.

Chapter 11: Fusion Recipes

Welcome to the exciting world of fusion recipes, where diverse culinary traditions come together to create something extraordinary. This chapter is all about experimenting with flavors and techniques from around the world, using your Traeger Grill to create dishes that are innovative, delicious, and uniquely your own. Imagine the spicy, smoky goodness of grilled tandoori chicken tacos or the savory delight of smoked teriyaki beef sliders. From grilled paneer tikka pizza to smoked Korean BBQ jackfruit sandwiches, these recipes blend the best of different cuisines into mouthwatering fusion dishes.

Each recipe is designed to showcase the versatility of your grill while bringing together unexpected flavors in a harmonious and delicious way. Get ready to embark on a culinary adventure that spans the globe, all from the comfort of your backyard.

11.1 Grilled Tandoori Chicken Tacos

Serves: 4

Cooking Time: 30 minutes

Temperature: 375°F

Grilled Tandoori Chicken Tacos borrow the idea of making chicken tandoori from the Indian culture while incorporating the elements of Mexican food preparation. Tender, delicious chicken is marinated, then cooked on a grill and wrapped in our warm flour tortillas, garnished with a tasteful sauce of yogurt and vegetables.

Ingredients:

- ➤ 4 boneless, skinless chicken breasts
- ➤ 1 cup plain Greek yogurt
- ➤ 2 tablespoons tandoori seasoning
- ➤ 1 tablespoon lemon juice
- ➤ 8 small flour tortillas
- ➤ 1 cup shredded lettuce
- ➤ 1 cup diced tomatoes
- ➤ 1/2 cup diced red onion
- ➤ 1/2 cup chopped fresh cilantro
- ➤ 1/2 cup plain Greek yogurt (for sauce)
- ➤ 1 tablespoon lime juice
- ➤ Salt and pepper to taste

Instructions:

- Combine your ¾ cup of brown sugar, 3 tablespoons of garlic powder, 1 teaspoon of paprika, and ¾ teaspoon of kosher salt. Mix it thoroughly. Next, place your 700-gram brisket on a wire rack over the foil. Massage the above mix equally on the fatty side of the brisket. After that, let it sit at room temperature for about an hour. Meanwhile, set your grill to 375°F.

- To prepare the marinade, firstly put the yogurt into a bowl, add the tandoori seasoning and lemon juice. Evenly spread the marinade on the chicken breasts and place chicken breasts in the dish. Add chicken and let it marinate for at least 30 minutes before cooking.

- Arrange the chicken breasts on the grill with the marinated side facing down Grill for 6 to 7 minutes then turn and grill for another 6 to 7 minutes or until it reaches 165°F.

- During preparing the time for cooking chicken, you need to prepare the toppings for the other products. For the sauce mix the Greek yogurt and lime juice in a small bowl also. Set aside.

- After preparing the chicken to be cooked, cut it into strips after it is done. Grill the tortillas for one minute on each side and prepare for serving. For each tort, layer a few strips of the chicken onto the tortilla, put shredded lettuce, diced tomatoes, diced red onions on top of it, and lastly chopped coriander. Finally, pour the yogurt-lime sauce over the cooked food and stir or mix gently.

- Top the tacos with the remaining sour cream and/or guacamole and serve the tacos immediately with some more lime wedges on the side.

Tips:

- To enhance taste, you should prevent the tortillas from being overly soft by grilling them slightly prior to their incorporation in the taco preparation.

- If you like your tandoori spices very spicy, you will need to adjust the seasoning to your preference.

11.2 Smoked Teriyaki Beef Sliders

Serves: 6

Cooking Time: 1 hour

Temperature: 225°F

Alay from savory, smokey essence of barbecue sauces, Smoked Teriyaki Beef Sliders have infused aspects of sweet and tangy Japanese teriyaki preparation methods. It is preferred as a party menu or just for a family, fun themed night dinner.

Ingredients:

- 1 pound ground beef
- 1/4 cup teriyaki sauce
- 1/4 cup panko breadcrumbs
- 1 egg
- 1 teaspoon garlic powder
- 1 teaspoon onion powder
- 1/2 teaspoon salt
- 1/4 teaspoon black pepper
- 6 slider buns
- 1/2 cup mayonnaise
- 1 tablespoon Sriracha
- 1 cup shredded lettuce
- 1/2 cup thinly sliced cucumbers

Instructions:

- Fat content in the meat helps it to stay moist during a long cooking process in the smoker intended to be set to 225 degrees Fahrenheit.

- To the bowl with the ground beef, add teriyaki sauce, panko breadcrumbs, eggs, garlic powder, onion powder, salt, and pepper. Mix until well combined. Divide the mixture into 6 portions and shape them into small oval cakes.

- The smoker grate should be used to grate the patties and smoke them for about 1 hour or until it registers 160°F internal temperature.

- They combined the mayonnaise and Sriracha chili sauce to form the spicy mayo sauce in a small bowl.

- For the sliders, take the buns and grill them. For this sandwich, one will need to place a smoked beef patty on each half of the bun, then add a spicy mayo, lettuce, and sliced cucumbers.

- It is recommendable to serve the sliders while they are hot, and in addition the spicy mayo can be served in a separate dish.

Tips:

- o If preferred, one can use ground turkey or chicken in place of the beef used in the preparation of the dish.

- o Down it with a side of grilled pineapple to introduce a true fusion element with an extra dimension of taste.

11.3 Smoked BBQ Pulled Pork Banh Mi

Serves: 6

Cooking Time: 6 hours

Temperature: 225°F

Smoked BBQ Pulled Pork Banh Mi is a truly innovative food idea that combines the smoky, meaty taste of American-style BBQ with the lightness of the Vietnamese food. It's a pleasant combination ideal for any sizzling grill aficionado searching for a new dish to add spice into his or her summer barbeque plan.

Ingredients:

- ➤ 3 pounds pork shoulder (Boston butt)
- ➤ 1/4 cup BBQ rub
- ➤ 1 cup BBQ sauce
- ➤ 6 French baguettes
- ➤ 1 cup pickled carrots and daikon
- ➤ 1/2 cup fresh cilantro leaves
- ➤ 1 jalapeño, thinly sliced
- ➤ 1/2 cup mayonnaise
- ➤ 1 tablespoon soy sauce
- ➤ 1 tablespoon lime juice

Instructions:

- Firstly, ensure your smoker cooker is well-prepared at a temperature of

225°F.

- Coat the pork shoulder with a BBQ rub and make sure it adheres to all the sides of the meat.

- Insert the pork shoulder into the smoker and continue to smoke for 6 hours until the internal temperature has reached 195°F, and the meat is succulent with ease.

- So, in a separate bowl, combine the mayo, soy sauce, and lime juice. Set aside.

- Pork shoulder must be removed from the smoker and reserved for 15-20 minutes to let the juices to set. When it is done take two forks to shred the pork and then add the barbecue sauce to the mixture.

- Cut the baguettes in lengthwise and spread out a layer of mayonnaise mixture on each side of the baguettes. Layer a liberal amount of the pork onto the roll, followed by the pickled vegetable mixture, cilantro leaves, and thinly sliced jalapeño.

- Spoon the vegetables onto the banh mi sandwiches and add extra BBQ sauce on the side and serve immediately.

Tips:

- Although it looks purely sandwich, you can also try adding a few slices of fresh cucumber to make it more natural and healthier.

- If these two forms of pickled carrots and daikon are not readily available in your store, you can come up with pickled carrots and daikon by using the following Ingredients: Warm water, cider vinegar, sugar, and salt.

11.4 Grilled Paneer Tikka Pizza

Serves: 4

Cooking Time: 15 minutes

Temperature: 450°F

Paneer tikka pizza Barbeque style is a blend of Paneer tikka's spicy, tangy taste with Pizza which results into a scrumptious dish appropriate for all occasions.

Ingredients:

> - 1 pound paneer, cubed
> - 1/2 cup plain yogurt
> - 2 tablespoons tikka masala paste
> - 1 teaspoon turmeric
> - 1 teaspoon garam masala
> - 2 pre-made pizza crusts
> - 1/2 cup pizza sauce
> - 2 cups shredded mozzarella cheese
> - 1 red onion, thinly sliced
> - 1 bell pepper, thinly sliced
> - Fresh cilantro leaves, for garnish

Instructions:

- It's also important to ensure that the grill has been pre-heated up to 450 degrees F.

- Mix the yogurt, tikka masala, turmeric and garam masala in a bowl and marinate the chicken for not less than 2-3 hours. Add the paneer cubes to the mixture and turn them gently to coat. It's advisable to leave it to marinate for approximately half an hour before cooking.

- Put the paneer pieces prepared with marination on skewers and barbeque for approximately ten minutes, each side, till the sides turn black as well as the paneer gets cooked inside.

- Tada, this means laying down a base of pizza sauce over each of the preeminent pizza bases. Finally, sprinkle with shredded mozzarella cheese before topping the pepperoni pizza with grilled paneer, slices of red onion and bell peppers.

- Arrange the pizzas on the grill and grill them for about 15-25 minutes until the cheese is thoroughly melted and the base of the pizza is crispy.

- Turn off the heat and take out the pizzas from the grill and garnish with fresh cilantro leaves. Slice and serve immediately.

Tips:

- To give the pizza a hot kick you may wish to rank this with some green chilies sliced and placed on the pizza as it is grilled.

- It served well with the homemade pizza dough if you can have the time to make your own dough for the pizza.

11.5 Korean BBQ Smoked Sandwich with Jackfruit

Serves: 6

Cooking Time: 1. 5 hours

Temperature: 225°F

Smoked Korean BBQ Jackfruit Sandwiches: This sandwich is a scrumptious plant-based recipe that is a healthier variation of the usual pulled pork sandwich; it has smoked jackfruit with Korean BBQ sauce served inside a toasted bun with a side of slaw.

Ingredients:

- 2 cans young jackfruit in brine, drained and rinsed
- 1 cup Korean BBQ sauce
- 6 sandwich buns
- 2 cups shredded cabbage
- 1/2 cup grated carrots
- 1/4 cup rice vinegar
- 1 tablespoon sesame oil
- 1 tablespoon soy sauce
- 1 tablespoon honey
- 1 teaspoon sesame seeds

Instructions:

- The ideal temperature for preparing this dish is 225°F, so preheat the smoker accordingly.

- Cut the jackfruit into pieces that are like the size of pork shreds. Pace the chicken and mix it with 1/2 cup Korean BBQ sauce.

- Arrange the cut jackfruit on the smoker tray and smoke for approximately 1. 5 hours, or until it has been properly seasoned with a smoky taste.

- Toss together the shredded cabbage, grated carrots, rice vinegar, sesame oil, soy sauce, honey, and sesame seeds in a large mixing bowl. Stir properly and then this preparation should be left to stand for some time before using.

- Grill the sandwich buns to give a crispy texture to the sandwiches. Put a double scoop of smoked jackfruit on each bun, follow up with a nice dollop of slaw.

- Korean BBQ served hot; accompany it with some extra Korean BBQ sauce.

Tips:

- o You can also add extra barbecue taste and soak the jackfruit in the barbecue sauce for over 24 hours before BBQ.

- o You can also incorporate some thinly sliced pieces of radish for extra crunchy and tang to the slaw.

11.6 Grilled Kimchi Quesadillas

Serves: 4

Cooking Time: 10 minutes

Temperature: 400°F

Grilled Kimchi Quesadillas is quite interesting combination of Korean kimchi and a typical Mexican quesadilla which not less delicious but quite different in a way.

Ingredients:

- ➢ 2 cups kimchi, chopped
- ➢ 2 cups shredded cheddar cheese
- ➢ 8 flour tortillas
- ➢ 1/4 cup sliced green onions
- ➢ 1/4 cup cilantro, chopped

> ➤ 1/4 cup sour cream (for serving)

Instructions:

- Using tongs, lightly oil the grill then turn your heat to high or set it at 400°F.

- Take four tortillas then make sure that you only put half of the shredded cheddar cheese, chopped kimchi, sliced green onions, and chopped cilantro on the top of the tortilla. Top it with the remaining tortillas.

- Arranging the quesadillas on the grilling surface, cook for 3-4 minutes, flipping over the tortillas occasionally until the cheese has melted and the tortillas crispy.

- Pull the quesadillas off the grill, divide the tortillas into drizzles, and accompany with a spear of sour cream.

Tips:

- o For an added boost, for an even more delicious quesadilla filing, you can mix some shredded cooked chicken or beef.

- o Additional kimchi should be served on the side for cattle those extra hot spice lovers.

11.7 Smoked Mediterranean Lamb Pita

Serves: 4

Cooking Time: 2 hours

Temperature: 225°F

The Smoked Mediterranean Lamb Pita has the perfect balance of spices that we associate with Mediterranean food, smokiness that comes from the meat and lamb, topped with fresh vegetables and a squeeze of tangy tzatziki sauce in a warm pita.

Ingredients:

> ➤ 2 pounds lamb shoulder, boneless
> ➤ 2 tablespoons Mediterranean seasoning

- ➢ 4 pita breads
- ➢ 1 cup tzatziki sauce
- ➢ 1 cup diced tomatoes
- ➢ 1 cup sliced cucumbers
- ➢ 1/2 cup red onion, thinly sliced
- ➢ 1/2 cup crumbled feta cheese
- ➢ Fresh mint leaves, for garnish

Instructions:

- Adjust your smoker temperature to 225 degrees Fahrenheit or 105 degrees Celsius.

- Using a piece of paper towel, pat the lamb shoulder dry, then rub the shoulder with mediterranean seasoning on all sides until well coated.

- Put the lamb onto the smoker and smoke it for around 2 hours or until it is tender, and the internal temperature is 63°C for those who prefer medium-rare.

- Take the lamb back from the smoker and allow it to relax before serving for 10-15 minutes. Slice the lamb thinly.

- Grill the pita breads to grill the pita breads you can warm them on the grill or toaster for like 20 seconds. Put a layer of tzatziki sauce, then put lamb slices, diced tomatoes, sliced cucumber, and red onion and eventually crumbled feta cheese on each pita.

- Sprinkle with fresh mint before serving or directly before eating the drink.

Tips:

- o For a chunkier meal, incorporate veneer grilled vegetables into the pita.

- o Grab a Greek yogurt and make your own tzatziki sauce – that will taste even better than anything store-bought.

11.8 Grilled Teriyaki Pineapple Burgers.

Serves: 4

Cooking Time: 15 minutes

Temperature: 400°F

Teriyaki Pineapple Burgers Grilled is quite a simple dish, and yet very exotic where juicy beef patties are united with sweet teriyaki glaze, grilled pineapple, or mango slices.

Ingredients:

- ➢ 1 pound ground beef
- ➢ 1/4 cup teriyaki sauce
- ➢ 4 pineapple rings
- ➢ 4 hamburger buns
- ➢ 4 slices Swiss cheese
- ➢ 1 cup shredded lettuce
- ➢ 1/4 cup mayonnaise
- ➢ 1 tablespoon soy sauce
- ➢ 1 teaspoon honey

Instructions:

- However, for the grilling process, you need your grill to be set to around 400°F.

- But before that, take one bowl and in that bowl combine the ground beef with at least 2 tablespoons of teriyaki sauce. To this, shape into four patties.

- Put the patties on the grill and grill for 5-6 minutes on each side or until the patties are done to the liking. In the later parts, place a slice of Swiss cheese on top of each patty to allow it to become melt.

- When the patties are on the grill, you should grill the pineapple slices for 2 minutes on each side of the pineapple to ensure that the pineapple slices have caramelized and grill marks on them.

- To prepare for the marinade, you need to combine the mayonnaise, soy sauce, and honey in a small sized bowl. Set aside.

- Grill the burger buns so that they have an appealing toasted crust. Place them on the buns and put a spoonful of sauce on each of them and a beef patty on the sauce, add the grilled pineapple ring and shredded lettuce.

- Take the burgers out of the grill and place them on wax paper while serving with additional the sauce on the side.

Tips:

- Optional, but to add flavor to the meat, soak patties in teriyaki sauce for at least half an hour prior to barbecuing them.

- Accompany with baked sweet potatoes, so it becomes a yummy dinner.

11.9 Smoked Italian Sausage Paella

Serves: 6

Cooking Time: 1. 5 hours

Temperature: 225°F

The combination of the smokiness of the American barbecue and the abundance of Spanish ingredients of the paella was the idea behind Smoked Italian Sausage Paella recipe that include smoked homemade sausage, saffron rice, and a variety of fresh vegetables.

Ingredients:

- 1 pound Italian sausage, sliced
- 2 cups Arborio rice
- 1 onion, finely chopped
- 1 red bell pepper, diced
- 1 yellow bell pepper, diced
- 1 cup green peas
- 4 cups chicken broth
- 1 teaspoon saffron threads
- 1 teaspoon smoked paprika
- 2 tablespoons olive oil
- 1 lemon, cut into wedges
- Fresh parsley, for garnish

Instructions:

- Start getting your smoker ready for cooking by preheating it to 225°F.

- In a big open pan or a cast iron fry pan, warm the olive oil on the medium setting. Also, I would like to add the sliced Italian sausage and cook for some time until browned. Sausage placement: take it out and put aside.

- Then, in the same pan, you need to add the chopped onion, the chopped red bell pepper, and the chopped yellow bell pepper as well. It is used to cook the vegetables until they turn soft.

- Pour in the Arborio rice and fry for 2-3 minutes while stirring the mixture to ensure the rice is evenly coated with the oil. Add the saffron threads and the smoked paprika and stir to incorporate.

- Pour in the chicken broth and let the combination come to boil. Place food in an oven or baking pan, then cover it with an aluminum foil.

- Put the pan inside the smoker and let it cook for an hour or one hour. And lastly, cook the rice for 5 hours or until the grains soften and are fully cooked with all the remaining liquid in the pot.

- To the pan, add the green peas and brown the sausage later and leave it for the last 10 minutes.

- Serve topped with freshly chopped parsley leaves and lemon slices to enhance the beauty of the cuisine. Serve immediately.

Tips:

o If you prefer a racier tasty, a spicy smoked shrimp or chicken might be suitable for the paella.

o I would suggest you use the best quality saffron for a better and enhanced taste of your dish.

11.10 Cajun Spice Mix

Serves: 4

Cooking Time: 10 minutes

Temperature: 400°F

Thai Peanut Satay Skewers are one of those appetizers that no Thai restaurant can do without – tender marinated chicken skewers grilled to nice chars and served with a delicious peanut sauce.

Ingredients:

- 2 pounds chicken breast, cut into strips
- 1/2 cup coconut milk
- 2 tablespoons soy sauce
- 1 tablespoon curry powder
- 1 teaspoon ground turmeric
- 1 teaspoon ground coriander
- 1/2 teaspoon ground cumin
- 1/2 teaspoon chili powder
- 1 cup peanut butter
- 1/4 cup soy sauce
- 1/4 cup lime juice
- 2 tablespoons honey
- 2 garlic cloves, minced
- 1/4 cup chopped peanuts (for garnish)
- Fresh cilantro, for garnish

Instructions:

- Prepare your grill for the grilling process with a temperature of around four hundred degrees.

- Pour all these marinades into a large bowl of coconut milk, soy sauce, curry powder, turmeric, coriander, cumin, and chili powder. Hi ladies Today am going to share one of my favorite dish Chicken tikka. Now mix well and add the chicken strips and marinate for at least 30 minutes.

- In one bowl, combine the peanut butter, soy sauce, lime juice, honey, and minced garlic for further use. Set aside.

- Pierce the chicken strips with the skewers and ensure that you marinade them properly. Arrange the skewers on the grill, and grill for 4-5 min on each side or until the chicken is tender and brown on one side.

- Are our tasty and the juicy grill chicken skewers ready, yes, let's serve it with the peanut sauce accompany with chopped peanuts and fresh cilantro.

Tips:

- When using wooden skewers, it is recommended that you soak them in water for at least 30 minutes before use to avoid burning them when grilling the food.

- For the vegetarian version of the suya, replace chicken with tofu or vegetables.

Chapter 12: Conclusion

Barbecue is not only a process but a way of expressing taste, the magical smell of food roasting and sharing epic moments. From the moment when the tasty delicacies ignite and sizzle on the hot folding grates to the moment when the taste and smell of burnt coal envelop the dish and become its part, grilling acts as a preparation that turns simple products into exquisite meals. I will end the book as a vital guide to the wide range of grilling possibilities, useful tips, tricks, and recipes for those who want to try something new in outdoor cooking experience. What you will notice from the chapters is that grilling can be done by those who want to get a certain kind of food and it is particularly suitable for those with specific tastes and those who have special diets. With everything from morning meals to evening delights and everything in-between, grilling involves wonderfully preparing, introduce volumes for you to consider. Every recipe has been well prepared to make sure that every time you prepare and cook a meal, it is both delicious and perfect.

Grilling is a technique that can be compared to any culinary art, as it requires the talent, feeling and understanding of the master. They fail to go beyond a simple outline of a recipe; they don't really explain how to control the heat on the grill and how to coax out the inherent taste in the beef. The process of grilling is, to a certain extent, primitive, but what sets grilling apart from other methods of preparing food is that it makes even the simplest of meals into events.

It has its own way of uniting people compared to any other social networking site. No matter it is a simple family dinner, a cheerful weekend party, or even a formal celebration of the New Year or any other significant event, the grill acts as an important supply in such events. For many, the process of grilling is not just about tasting the product, but it can bring together people throughout varying stages such as preparing the grill and savoring the result. Although this book does not cover all different types of ceremonies and traditions, it has been a good guide to a variety of grilling style and dishes. What makes grilling so exciting is the versatility of the process and you can easily modify things to your preferences once you are confident with your skills. Experiment with a variety of wood chips or pellets until you find the ones that taste best to you. I mean that you can change the type of Seasoning additions and marinades according to your preferences. There are numerous things to try, and the grill is the plate you have to paint on! Cooking at barbeque also has its merits and it can be considered a sort of healthy cooking since the fats can easily melt off food and the nutrients are not 'cooked-out' as they may be when the food is cooked for long, at high temperatures. Despite the use of rich sauces and creamy gravies, many of the recipes in this book prominently feature fresh vegetables, lean meats, and fish, making them healthy food options for the dinner table. The breakdown of a number of components coupled with the uses of grill allows one to have a balanced diet in view of the numerous benefits associated with Barbeque food.

Before deciding the path, you are going to follow in the grilling process you have to consider the consequences you are going to cause to the environment. When possible, focus on buying local, organic, and free-range produce because they have less chemicals and cruelty. Discover some plant-based dishes to help fight climate change more actively and learn how one can live a greener life. Grilling is all about enjoying the natural gifts that are bestowed upon by the mother earth and for this, we need to understand that we should not spoil the earth for our future generations.

Grilling is always an ever- rolling stream and yet the change is always for the better with new inventions and more sophisticated methods being adopted. In conclusion, remember to remain passionate and eager to discover the differences in the tastes and contrast in flavors when using other types of grills, when attempting new recipes, and when introducing the new gadgets in the grilling process. Grilling means barbecuing and the future has a lot to offer, and it is always fascinating to look at new possibilities. To sum it up, this book is not just a 'recipe' book; it is a guide to grilling and a promise of the wonders that this cooking technique can bring, whether one is cooking indoors or outdoors. It is about flavors that come with grilling, the trial, and learning process or even the pleasure of knowing that what is in the grill is enough to feed everyone. As you turn to these pages and light the charcoal, you need to understand that grilling is not just about food, but the love that it takes to prepare it.

That concludes the flavor profile guide. Thank you for tuning in and participating in this foodie adventure. We want you to become the grill master who will grab whatever is available and start cooking on the grill with enthusiasm. Bon appétit, dear friends! May you enjoy the dishes that come out of your grill for many more years to come.

12. 1 Conversions Chart

In cooking, measurements can be sensitive to detail and, when changing from one unit to another, it can be useful to have accessible equations. Below shows some typical conversion tables, using which will assist you in the translation of one unit of measurement to another with ease.

Volume Conversions

1 teaspoon (tsp) = 1/3 tablespoon (tbsp)
1 tablespoon (tbsp) = 3 teaspoons (tsp)
1 cup (c) = 16 tablespoons (tbsp)
1 pint (pt) = 2 cups (c)
1 quart (qt) = 2 pints (pt)
1 gallon (gal) = 4 quarts (qt)
1 milliliter (ml) = 0.034 fluid ounces (fl oz)
1 liter (l) = 1000 milliliters (ml) = 33.814 fluid ounces (fl oz)

Weight Conversions

1 ounce (oz) = 28.35 grams (g)
1 pound (lb) = 16 ounces (oz)
1 kilogram (kg) = 1000 grams (g) = 2.20462 pounds (lb)
Temperature Conversions
Fahrenheit (°F) to Celsius (°C): (°F - 32) × 5/9 = °C
Celsius (°C) to Fahrenheit (°F): (°C × 9/5) + 32 = °F
Common Cooking Temperatures
Low: 200-300°F (93-149°C)
Medium: 300-375°F (149-190°C)
High: 375-450°F (190-232°C)
Broil: 450-550°F (232-288°C)
Dry Ingredient Conversions
1 cup flour = 120 grams (g)
1 cup sugar = 200 grams (g)
1 cup brown sugar (packed) = 220 grams (g)
1 cup powdered sugar = 120 grams (g)
1 cup butter = 227 grams (g)

12.2 Index

Beef Ribs, Smoked: 5.4
Beef Tri-Tip Roast, Smoked: 5.8
Brisket, Classic Smoked: 5.1
Breakfast Burritos, Grilled: 2.4
Breakfast Casserole, Smoked: 2.7
Breakfast Pizza, Grilled: 2.10
Brussels Sprouts, Grilled: 8.9
Burgers, Smoked: 5.6
Brownies, Smoked: 9.6

C
Calamari, Grilled: 7.1
Cajun Spice Mix: 10.10
Cauliflower Steaks, Smoked: 8.4
Cheddar Cheese Balls, Smoked: 3.7
Chicken Breasts, Grilled: 4.2
Chicken Drumsticks, Smoked: 4.8
Chicken Thighs, Grilled: 4.5
Chicken Tenders, Smoked: 4.10
Chicken Wings with BBQ Sauce, Grilled: 4.9
Chicken Wings, Smoked: 3.1
Chocolate Chip Cookies, Grilled: 9.1
Clams, Grilled: 7.8
Corn on the Cob, Grilled: 8.5
Cornish Hens, Grilled: 4.7

D
Deviled Eggs, Smoked: 3.5
Duck, Smoked: 4.4

E
Eggplant Parmesan, Smoked: 8.6

F
Flatbread with Toppings, Grilled: 3.8
Flank Steak, Grilled: 5.5
French Toast, Grilled: 2.2
Frittata, Smoked: 2.9

G
Garlic Herb Butter: 10.4

H
Ham, Smoked: 6.5

Q
Queso Dip, Smoked: 3.3

R
Ribeye Steaks, Grilled: 5.2
Ribs, Grilled BBQ: 6.10
Ribs, Smoked Baby Back: 6.3
Ribs, Smoked Beef: 5.4

S
Sausage and Hash Browns, Smoked: 2.3
Sausage Links, Smoked: 6.7
Shrimp Skewers, Grilled: 7.2
Smoked Chicken Tenders: 4.10
S'mores, Grilled: 9.3
Sausage Paella, Smoked Italian: 11.9
Scallops, Grilled: 7.6
Sausage Links, Smoked: 6.7
Skewers, Grilled Vegetable: 8.3
S'mores, Grilled: 9.3
Stuffed Mushrooms, Grilled: 3.6
Stuffed Peppers, Smoked: 8.2
Sweet Corn, Grilled: 8.5
S'mores, Grilled: 9.3

T
T-Bone Steaks, Grilled: 5.9
Teriyaki Beef Sliders, Smoked: 11.2
Teriyaki Marinade, Asian: 10.6
Teriyaki Pineapple Pizza, Grilled: 11.8
Tandoori Chicken Tacos, Grilled: 11.1
Tomato Soup, Smoked: 8.8
Tuna Steaks, Grilled: 7.4
Turkey Breast Roast: 4.3
Turkey Legs, Smoked: 4.6

V
Vegetable Skewers, Grilled: 8.3

Z
Zucchini Fries, Grilled: 3.10

Made in United States
Troutdale, OR
12/18/2024